SHOVEL BUM

This book is dedicated to all the hardworking shovel bums of the world. The shovel bum's lot is a difficult one and those who somehow manage to make a long-term career of it deserve our respect.

SHOVEL BUM

COMIX OF ARCHAEOLOGICAL FIELD LIFE

Carpe per Diem

Shovel Bum

Trent de Boer

ALTAMIRA
PRESS

A Division of
ROWMAN & LITTLEFIELD PUBLISHERS, INC.
Walnut Creek • Lanham • New York • Oxford

AltaMira Press
A Division of Rowman & Littlefield Publishers, Inc.
1630 North Main Street, #367
Walnut Creek, CA 94596
http://www.altamirapress.com

Rowman & Littlefield Publishers, Inc.
A Member of the Rowman & Littlefield Publishing Group
4501 Forbes Blvd, Suite 200
Lanham, MD 20706

PO Box 317
Oxford
OX2 9RU, United Kingdom

British Library Cataloguing in Publication Information Available

Library of Congress Cataloging-in-Publication Data

de Boer, Trent.
  Shovel bum : comix of archaeological field life / Trent de Boer.
       p.   cm.
  Includes bibliographical references.
  ISBN 0-7591-0682-7 (pbk. : alk. paper)
  1. Archaeology—Field work.   I. Title.
CC76.D35   2004
930.1—dc22
                                        2004008220

Printed in the United States of America

♾™ The paper used in this publication meets the minimum requirements of American National Standard for Information Sciences—Permanence of Paper for Printed Library Materials, ANSI/NISO Z39.48—1992.

Contents

ACKNOWLEDGMENTS

Shovel Bum would not exist without the contributors, so I want to give a special thanks to each and every one of them. A quick scan of this book's Table of Contents shows just how vital these contributors are to the diversity found in each *Shovel Bum* issue. A big thanks goes to my partner in crime, Betsy de Boer, whose cover art, comix, and spot illustrations define the *Shovel Bum* aesthetic. I'd like to thank Mitch Allen for his encouragement and support. Mitch convinced me that a book version of *Shovel Bum* could work, regardless of the lo-fi quality of much of the original *Shovel Bum* artwork. Thanks also to those who have worked with me and had to see their crude caricatures in my stories. If anyone feels I have portrayed him or her in a bad—and in some cases disfiguring—light, I apologize. Finally, thanks go to the loyal *Shovel Bum* readers. I appreciate all of the feedback and compliments you've sent me over the years.

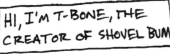

HI, I'M T-BONE, THE CREATOR OF SHOVEL BUM

HEY!

I STARTED SHOVEL BUM IN 1997 TO SHOW MY FAMILY & FRIENDS WHAT MY WIFE BETSY AND I DID FOR WORK.

HOW ABOUT A CRM COMIC BOOK?

THE FIRST ISSUE WAS A "DAY-IN-THE-LIFE" OF A SHOVEL BUM.

HOW DO I DRAW A TRANSECT?

WE WORKED IN ARKANSAS AT THE TIME AND FOUND PLENTY OF GOOD FODDER

REMEMBER THAT HILLBILLY WHO CAME AT US WITH A PISTOL?

AFTER MOVING TO SEATTLE, I STARTED READING A LOT OF SELF-PUBLISHED COMICS AND STORIES (ZINES).

GENIUS!

KING CAT

THIS INSPIRED ME TO EXPAND THE SCOPE & SOLICIT CONTRIBUTIONS FROM LIKE-MINDED SHOVEL BUMS.

SHOVEL BUM

SHOVEL BUM GREW INTO A FORUM FOR DISCUSSING THE UNIQUE FIELD LIFESTYLE.

NO SUBJECT IS OFF LIMITS.

IN THE NEXT ISSUE, I WILL REVEAL MY SECRET PICKLED EGG RECIPE!

THE DIVERSE SUBMISSIONS FROM SHOVEL BUMS ACROSS THE COUNTRY MAKES FOR A GOOD READ.

AT LEAST I THINK SO!

THEMED ISSUES BEGAN WITH ISSUE #3. SINCE THEN, WE'VE LOOKED AT BAD MOTELS, FIELD VEHICLES, MILITARY WORK, AND MORE.

FUTURE THEMES: MONITORING, ALASKA, AND CORPORATE ARCHAEOLOGY.

IN ADDITION TO GREAT SUBMISSIONS, WE ALSO GET HILARIOUS LETTERS TO THE EDITOR.

THIS GUY SAYS HE STAYED IN A MOTEL BUILT IN AN OLD SWIMMING POOL!

MOST OF SHOVEL BUM'S CONTENT IS HUMOROUS. SOMETIMES A SENSE OF HUMOR IS THE ONLY THING TO GET YOU THOUGH THE DAY.

HA HA, IT'S 7AM AND YER ALREADY SOAKED!

SO ARE YOU.

BEING A SHOVEL BUM AIN'T EASY → THERE'S NO JOB SECURITY, THE WORK IS TOUGH, AND OFTEN THE PAY IS BAD.

YOU GOTTA LOVE ARCHAEOLOGY TO LAST IN THIS FIELD.

"TRUE" SHOVEL BUMS GO PROJECT TO PROJECT & USUALLY MISS OUT ON THE POST-FIELD TASKS.

NEXT JOB

THE FOLKS WHO HELP MAKE A PROJECT SUCCESSFUL OFTEN AREN'T AROUND WHEN THE PROJECT IS COMPLETED.

BOY, I SURE WISH THE CREW WAS HERE TO ENJOY THIS PARTY

THIS BOTHERS ME & I'VE TRIED TO HONOR THE HARD WORKING SHOVEL BUMS OF THE WORLD WITH EACH ISSUE.

SHOVEL BUMS UNITE!

THIS BOOK COLLECTS THE BEST OF THE FIRST 8 ISSUES OF SHOVEL BUM.

THE COLLECTED WORKS OF
SHOVEL BUM

THE CHAPTERS ARE ARRANGED THEMATICALLY, NOT CHRONOLOGICALLY.

THE S.B. PURISTS ARE GONNA KILL ME.

INCLUDED AT THE START OF EACH CHAPTER ARE BETSY'S ORIGINAL COVER DESIGNS.

TAKE A BOW BETSY.

ALSO INCLUDED IN THE BOOK IS AN AFTERWORD BY FREQUENT CONTRIBUTOR TROY LOVATA.

AMONG OTHER THINGS, TROY DISCUSSES THE ZINE PHENOMENA, SO START THERE IF YOU'RE CURIOUS.

zine (zeen) n.
a self published paper covered illustr... periodical containi... ...ticles or stori... ...writers

SHOVEL BUM IS ON-GOING, WITH NEW ISSUES EACH YEAR

IT TAKES A WHILE TO GET ENOUGH MATERIAL

IF YOU WOULD LIKE TO CONTRIBUTE, E-MAIL: DUTCHCIRCUS@HOTMAIL.COM

I HOPE YOU ENJOY THIS BOOK AS MUCH AS I'VE ENJOYED PUTTING IT TOGETHER

LEMME KNOW WHAT YOU THINK OF IT!

Chapter 1

ARKANSAS

Arkansas, Trent de Boer
Letters, Trent de Boer, Betsy de Boer
Cover Art: Betsy de Boer

Since *Shovel Bum* was "born" in Arkansas, it seems a fitting place to start this book. Arkansas remains the most difficult place I've ever done archaeology. There are so many factors that make the shovel bum life difficult in Arkansas: high humidity and heat, poorly managed forests, steep ridges, and a multitude of nasty critters. Wages aren't especially high in Arkansas, so shovel bum jobs there often pay much less than in other parts of the country. Still, the hardships of the Arkansas shovel bum life produced a wealth of good stories.

WE STAY AT MOTELS IN SMALL TOWNS NEAR OUR SURVEY AREAS. LATELY WE'VE BEEN STAYING AT THE BULL'S MOTEL — IT'S RUN BY TWO OLD PEOPLE.

AT ONE OF THE OTHER MOTELS WE STAY AT, THEY GIVE US FREE BISCUITS AND GRAVY AND COFFEE FOR BREAKFAST!

NOT TOO MUCH GRAVY FOR ME.

AFTER A HEARTY BREAKFAST, WE ALL GET INTO OUR CREWS AND HEAD OUT TO OUR SURVEY AREAS. WE DRIVE A JEEP, A FEW TOYOTAS, AND AN OLD NISSAN.

RED JEEP   GREEN TOYOTA   NISSAN   TOYOTA T100

WHEN WE GET TO OUR SURVEY AREAS, WE GRAB OUR GEAR AND START SURVEYING. THE MAIN GOAL IS FOR US TO FIND SITES — HISTORIC AND PREHISTORIC. WE DIG SHOVEL TESTS TO FIND SITES.

WHEN WE FIND A SITE (IT COULD BE A PIECE OF GLASS OR A NAIL TO TELL US A HISTORIC SITE IS THERE, OR A PROJECTILE POINT INDICATING A PREHISTORIC SITE), WE ALL GO CRAZY.

ARROWHEAD!!

ALL THE OTHER CREW MEMBERS COME OFF THEIR TRANSECTS AND WE TEST THE SITE. WE SHOVEL TEST IT, LOOK FOR ABOVE-THE-GROUND FEATURES, AND DETERMINE ITS EXTENT.

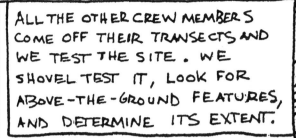

PLEASE DIG A SHOVEL TEST AT 10M SOUTH, 20M EAST O'CREW

ONE PERSON IS IN CHARGE OF RECORDING THE SITE: MAPPING IT, KEEPING TRACK OF THE ARTIFACTS RECOVERED, PLOTTING THE SITE ON A TOPO MAP, FLAGGING THE SITE WITH ORANGE & BLACK TAPE, ETC.

HMM, IT LOOKS LIKE THE SLOPE RISES THERE TO THE NORTH

ONCE THE SITE HAS BEEN COMPLETELY RECORDED AND THE PERIMETER HAS BEEN FLAGGED OFF WITH THE PROTECTION TAPE (IF WE DEEM IT WORTHY), WE ALL HEAD BACK TO OUR TRANSECTS TO CONTINUE OUR SURVEYING.

BYE BYE

ONE OF THE THINGS I LIKE ABOUT SURVEYING IS THAT IT GIVES ME A LOT OF TIME TO THINK ABOUT ALL SORTS OF THINGS.

ANOTHER THING THAT IS NICE ABOUT SURVEYING IS THAT WE GET TO DRINK LOTS OF GATORADE.

	POISON IVY	BRIARS
BUT BEING A SHOVEL BUM IN ARKANSAS IS NOT ALL FUN AND GAMES. THERE ARE A LOT OF NASTY PLANTS AND CREATURES THAT MAKE LIFE VERY UNPLEASANT AT TIMES. SOME OF THESE INCLUDE:	"LEAVES OF 3, LEAVE THEM BE"	

SEED TICKS	LONE STAR TICKS	ROCKY MOUNTAIN SPOTTED FEVER TICKS	MOSQUITOS	GNATS

CHIGGERS	NO-SEE-UMS	SCORPIONS	BLACK WIDOW	OUACHITA MOUNTAIN SPIDERS

DADDY LONGLEGS	WATER SPIDERS	DONNER BUGS	WATER MOCCASINS	DIAMOND BACKS

RATTLERS	COPPERHEADS	BLACK RACERS	GREEN VINE SNAKES	PYGMIE RATTLERS

BLACK BEARS	ARMADILLOS (CAUSE LEPROSY)	COYOTES	SKUNKS	HILLBILLIES

ALTHOUGH HILLBILLIES CAN BE A SERIOUS NUISANCE, (EVER SEEN "DELIVERANCE"?) THE REAL THREAT IS OFTEN PRIVATE PROPERTY OWNERS WHO LIVE ADJACENT TO OUR SURVEY AREAS. OFTEN, THESE FOLKS ARE SIMPLY WORRIED ABOUT THEIR SECRET MARIJUANA CROPS HIDDEN AWAY IN THE NATIONAL FOREST.

WE HAD ONE GUY COME OUT AND REALLY TRY TO INTIMIDATE US, EVEN THOUGH WE WERE IN THE NATIONAL FOREST.

I TOLD HIM WHAT WE WERE DOING AND HOW WE HAD A GOVERNMENT CONTRACT TO WORK ON.

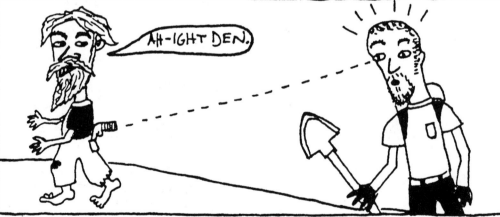

THE GUY WAS NICE TO US AFTER WE TOLD HIM WHY WE WERE THERE, BUT I NOTICED A PISTOL IN HIS BACK POCKET AS HE WALKED AWAY!

SOME FOLKS ARE VERY MEAN

OTHER FOLKS ARE JUST CURIOUS AND FRIENDLY

BUT WHEN THE ALARM CLOCK GOES OFF THE NEXT MORNING, IT'S BACK TO THE GRINDSTONE.

WE EAT A BREAKFAST OF POPTARTS, JUICE, AND COFFEE AND HEAD OUT AGAIN.

I SURE WISH I WAS EATING BISCUITS AND GRAVY.

THIS SUMMER WE'VE BEEN WORKING EXCLUSIVELY ON OUR OUACHITA NATIONAL FOREST SURVEY CONTRACT. IT'S A BIG CONTRACT AND SPEARS HAS BEEN WORKING ON IT FOR SEVERAL YEARS. ALL THE HRT'S (HERITAGE RESOURCE TECHNICIANS) FOR THE FOREST SERVICE KNOW US.

HELLO BEN

HELLO T-BONE

HELLO T-BONE

WHY HELLO RICHARD

WORKING IN THE OUACHITAS IS PRETTY NICE; IT'S A BEAUTIFUL PLACE TO SPEND YOUR DAY. BUT IT'S A LOT OF UP-AND-DOWN HIKING AND IT CAN GET TO BE PRETTY TIRING ON A 100+ DEGREE DAY.

PEOPLE SEEMED TO BE INTERESTED IN THE STORIES OF THE HUMBLE SHOVEL BUM, SO WE DECIDED TO DO SOME MORE OF THEM

IF THERE'S ONE THING A SHOVEL BUM HAS, IT'S STORIES

THIS TIME AROUND, I THOUGHT I'D TAP INTO SOME OF THE GREAT WEALTH OF STORIES THAT HAVE OCCURRED IN THIS GREAT STATE OF ARKANSAS.

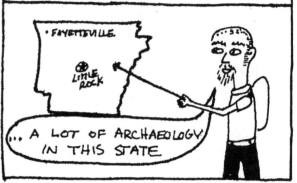

... A LOT OF ARCHAEOLOGY IN THIS STATE

WORKING FOR SPEARS INC. HAS REALLY EXPOSED ME TO A LOT OF ARKANSAS, NOT JUST THE OUACHITA MOUNTAINS.

HEADING DOWN TO TEXARKANA

FOR ME, BEING FROM THE NORTH, TEXARKANA WAS MY FIRST EXPOSURE TO THE "REAL" SOUTH. I SAW MANY STRANGE THINGS.

AWW MAN, THAT GUY'S DRINKING THE JUICE FROM A VIENNA SAUSAGE TIN!

THE HEAT AND HUMIDITY IN THE SOUTHERN PORTION OF THE STATE TOOK A LONG TIME TO GET USED TO, A LONG TIME.

HOW CAN IT BE 95 DEGREES AT 7 AM ?!!

BUT I THINK THE WORST PART OF IT WERE THOSE DAMN TEXARKANA BRIARS. THEY WERE THE THICKEST THINGS YOU'VE EVER SEEN. IN SOME CASES, IT WAS IMPOSSIBLE TO GET THROUGH.

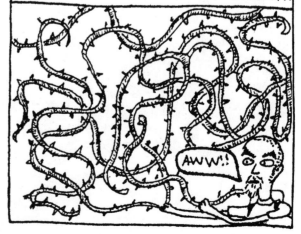

AWW!!

WE WERE WORKING DOWN IN TEXARKANA ON THE BIG HIGHWAY 71 PROJECT. THEY'RE TRYING TO MAKE ARKANSAS MORE ACCESSIBLE TO THE REST OF THE COUNTRY WITH A NEW INTERSTATE.

HEY MA, THOSE CARS JUST KEEP A COMIN'!

NOT EVERYONE IS HAPPY ABOUT LOSING THEIR LAND TO THE NEW SUPER HIGHWAY. WE GET CAUGHT IN THE MIDDLE — HAVING TO GO AND SURVEY THEIR LAND.

COME ON YOU GUYS, I DON'T WANT THAT GUY COMING DOWN & BUGGING US!

ME AND TWO OTHER WORKERS WERE WALKING ACROSS THIS GUY'S PROPERTY TO SURVEY PART OF THE HIGHWAY'S PROPOSED CORRIDOR.

OFF IN THE DISTANCE WE SAW A POND WITH A ROWBOAT IN IT. AS WE GOT CLOSER, WE NOTICED THERE WERE TWO GIRLS IN IT WEARING NO TOPS!

WHOA!!

BEFORE WE COULD GET A CLOSER LOOK, THE GUY WHO OWNED THE LAND STARTED YELLING AT US TO COME OVER TO HIM.

THESE ARE SHOVELS!

WHY YOU GOT GUNS ON MY PROPERTY?!!

BY THE TIME WE HAD EXPLAINED THINGS AND GOT BACK TO THE POND, THE GIRLS HAD PUT THEIR TOPS ON.

AWW JEEZ!!

A LOT OF THE LAND OWNERS WERE PRETTY HELPFUL AND OFTEN PROVIDED US WITH USEFUL INFORMATION.

NOW OVER THERE USED TO BE AN OLD BARN...

USUALLY THESE PEOPLE WOULD HAVE AN INTEREST IN ARCHAEOLOGY. SOMETIMES THEY WOULD INVITE US OVER AND SHOW US THEIR ARROWHEAD COLLECTIONS.

THIS HERE'S MY PRIDE AND JOY. I FOUND ALL THESE ARROWHEADS MYSELF AND GLUED 'EM ON.

YEAH, REAL NICE

YEAH, TEXARKANA IS A FUNNY PLACE. ONE DAY I WAS DOING SOME SHOVEL TESTS AND I SAW A 10 FOOT SNAKE.

THE SHOVEL BUM LIFESTYLE CAN BE A DIFFICULT ONE. IT IS ESPECIALLY EVIDENT WHEN YOU ARE FORCED TO LODGE WITH VIRTUAL STRANGERS

SO, WHO'S SLEEPING WHERE?

ALL I KNOW IS I'M GETTING A BED.

YAH, YAH, AWW!!!

HUH?!!

ONE NIGHT WE WERE AWAKENED BY THE UNHOLY SCREAMING OF OUR YOUNG COMRADE.

* INSERT YOUR NAME

THE BAD THING ABOUT THE BACKSTABBING IS THAT IT OFTEN RESULTS IN PEOPLE GETTING LAID OFF.

SOMETIMES YOU CAN FIND ANOTHER JOB WITH A DIFFERENT CONTRACT COMPANY IN THE AREA, OTHER TIMES IT'S THE UNEMPLOYMENT OFFICE FOR YOU.

THERE ARE A LOT OF SHOVEL BUMS OUT THERE WHO LOOK AT THESE UNEMPLOYMENT PERIODS AS THEIR YEARLY VACATION TIME.

OTHERS DEVELOP SUCH A STRONG WORK ETHIC THAT COLLECTING UNEMPLOYMENT IS NOT AN OPTION.

ON A GOOD DAY, YOU REALIZE WHY YOU PUT UP WITH IT.

There's nothing quite like doing archaeology.

Steady... Steady...

Being up on some remote ridgetop, looking down upon the world, is very exhilarating.

Can you believe they pay me for this?

Nice thing is, they're doing archaeology all over this big ol' country of ours.

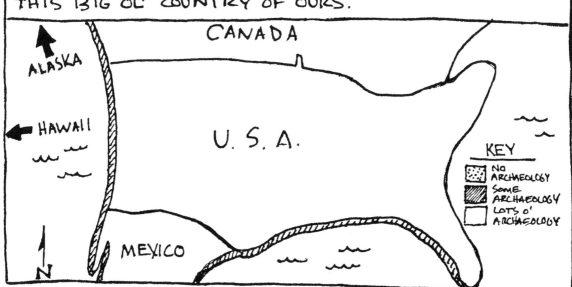

So we decided it was time to see more of the country.

Let's do it!

We packed up the car and headed west, to... Washington state!

The end?

Letters

Dear Shovel Bum,
My husband and I were taking a scenic drive on the newly finished Highway 71 through Mena, Arkansas, when we stumbled across a quaint little watering hole called "The Fish Net." We stopped in to wet our whistle and were both impressed by the "Arkansas Martini." Could *Shovel Bum* acquire the recipe?

Thirstin' in Thurston County

Dear Thirstin',
The fine folks at the Fish Net were a bit reluctant to divulge their recipe at first. You see, Mena's in a dry county and you shouldn't have been able to get a drink with any kick whatsoever. But with a little prodding, the famed Arkansas Martini formula is ours!

The Arkansas Martini
8 oz. Moonshine, chilled
1 pickled egg
Strain moonshine for any "floaters."
Pour quickly into a Mason canning jar.
Serve with pickled egg for garnish.
Bon Appetit!

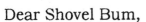

THIS MARTINI TASTES LIKE BURNING

Dear Shovel Bum,
My buddy and I want you to settle an argument—he thinks that CRM companies should provide the crew with all the tools they'll use on a project, including basics like trowels, tape measures, and even compasses. I think that a real shovel bum should already own all that stuff. What do you think?

Taking Pride

Dear Taking Pride,
I hope you put money on that argument, because that money is yours. Just like a mechanic owns his own wrenches and a tattoo artist owns his own guns, so should a shovel bum own his own dig kit. Sure, CRM companies are to be expected to provide tools like the transit, screens and shovels, the field vehicle, and so on, but a true shovel bum will not stray far from his dig kit. Isn't this common knowledge?!!

Chapter 2

FOOD

In the field, no other topic is as widely discussed as food. Before breakfast has been digested, you're already thinking about lunch. What's for dinner is a frequent lunchtime conversation. Per diem certainly factors into these decisions, as projects with higher per diem allow for carne asada, while projects with low per diem may only allow for bean burritos. To date, the food topic has only barely been touched on in *Shovel Bum* and a future issue devoted entirely to field food is in the works.

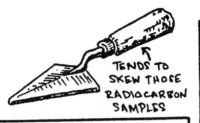

TENDS TO SKEW THOSE RADIOCARBON SAMPLES

DEAR TO MY HEART IS THE TIME WE USED A TROWEL TO FLIP STEAKS COOKED ON A CAMPFIRE USING A DRY SCREEN AS A GRILL.

MANY A SAVVY CREW CHIEF KNOWS THE VALUE OF A 10:30 DONUT BREAK OR THE OCCASIONAL CHILLED WATER-MELON TO APPEASE THE LABOR FORCE.

DIG = HAPPY

WORK IS GOOD!

CAFE

20 U.S. THE OF A 20
A
TWE'Y
MOVE DIRT JACK DIG
20 TWENTY BUCKS 20

USUALLY SHOVEL BUMS GET $20 OR $30 PER DIEM AND FEND FOR THEMSELVES.

BREAKFAST IS FREE AT THE HOTEL, LUNCH IS BROWN BAG & ONLY $6 FOR DINNER, INCLUDING THIS DRINK!

THIS CAN BE QUITE PROFITABLE

BUT THERE CAN BE A DOWN SIDE...

ONCE I WORKED IN A SMALL ROCKY MTN. TOWN WITH ONLY 4 PLACES TO EAT...

WHEN YOU'RE HERE, YOU'RE FAMILY!

"VINNY" THE WAITER

TO MAKE MATTERS WORSE, ONE PLACE HAD IFFY FOOD AND WAS RUN BY A HONCHO FROM LAS VEGAS WHO WAS RUMORED TO HAVE MOB CONNECTIONS!

BUT WE HAD TO EAT THERE 'CUZ WE WERE PAID PER DIEM IN $100 BILLS AND THE MAFIOSO WAS THE ONLY ONE WHO COULD MAKE CHANGE FOR TWO DOZEN SHOVEL BUMS.

MOTEL 6

HERE'S YOUR CHANGE, ANYTHING ELSE? A BET ON THE HORSES? A HIGH INTEREST PERSONAL LOAN?

NOTICE THE PINKY RING

A WHILE IN THE FIELD, WHETHER IN A TENT OR MOTEL, AND YOU BEGIN TO REALLY MISS THE HOME COOKING.

BY FAR MY STRANGEST ARCHAEO-GASTRONOMIC EXPERIENCE HAPPENED WHILE WORKING ALONG THE RIO GRANDE...

WE SPENT EIGHT HOURS A DAY WALKING TRANSECTS IN THE BLAZING AUGUST SUN.

THE BURNING SUN AND LACK OF RAIN FALL DROPPED RESERVOIR LEVELS AND EXPOSED LOTS OF REALLY NIFTY ARCHAEOLOGY FOR US SHOVEL BUMS TO UNCOVER.

EXTRA NICE POINT

WORKING HARD AT 105° FARENHIET MEANT THAT EVEN IF YOU DRANK A GALLON AND A HALF OF GATORADE AND ICED TEA, YOU ONLY HAD TO PEE ONCE A DAY!

TASTES LIKE SYRUP, BUT GOOD FOR YA'

TWIST O'LEMON, NO SUGAR

WITH ALL THIS YOU'D EXPECT US TO BE EMACIATED AS SHIP-WRECK SURVIVORS...

TRANSITIONAL ARCHAIC.

PRE-CLOVIS.

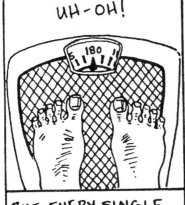

UH-OH!

BUT EVERY SINGLE CREW MEMBER GAINED WEIGHT!

THE BOSS WOULDN'T PAY US CASH PER DIEM, INSTEAD HE'D REIMBURSE US FOR FOOD RECEIPTS.

NEIN! ¡SÍ!

TO WEAK FOR WORK

BUT CAN PAY RENT

98 lb. WEAK LING

THE BOSS MAN SAID THAT SHOVEL BUMS WERE TOO WEAK TO WORK 'CUZ THEY SAVED PER DIEM INSTEAD OF BUYING FOOD.

THE BOSS WASN'T A COMPLETE SLAVE DRIVER. HIS COMPROMISE WAS TO PAY FOR ANY FOOD RECEIPT, NO MATTER WHAT IT WAS OR WHAT IT HAD COST!

"DINNER FOR ONE"

CONSEQUENTLY, WE HAD A LOT OF SHRIMP COCKTAIL APPETIZERS AND BIG, JUICY STEAK DINNERS. WE HAD A LOT OF EVERYTHING.

BUT, THESE DAYS I'M IN GRADUATE SCHOOL AND GOING INTO THE FIELD IS MORE LIKE A VACATION THAN SHOVEL BUM WORK.

BUT ATTENDING GRADUATE SCHOOL FOR AN ADVANCED DEGREE IN ARCHAEOLOGY HOLDS FOOD PARADOXES OF ALL ITS OWN!

SPENT FOOD MONEY ON TEXT BOOKS

ARCH
RENFREW
M SAHLINS
ARCH 101

YOU'RE EITHER TOO POOR TO BUY SUFFICIENT NOURISHMENT...

HAVE A TWINKIE DAVE...

HAL 9000

... OR YOU GET PLUMP FROM SITTING IN THE LIBRARY OR IN FRONT OF A COMPUTER ALL DAY.

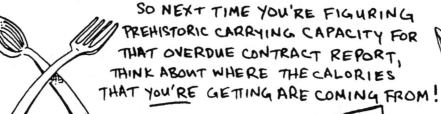

SO NEXT TIME YOU'RE FIGURING PREHISTORIC CARRYING CAPACITY FOR THAT OVERDUE CONTRACT REPORT, THINK ABOUT WHERE THE CALORIES THAT YOU'RE GETTING ARE COMING FROM!

THE END.

ONE DAY SHOVEL BUM FELT A BIT PECKISH AFTER A COUPLE BOTTLES OF BEER. HE EYED HIS OPTIONS...

chips?

jerky?

peanuts?

egg?

EGG.

50¢

saltines

chopped onions

egg

OH MY LORD

MUCH TO HIS SURPRISE, IT WAS A BOUNTIFUL BASKET, NOT JUST AN EGG ON A NAPKIN. PERFECTLY HARD BOILED AND DELICATELY SEASONED - IT WAS THE FOOD OF GODS!

T-Bone's Old Fashioned Pickled Eggs

I've decided it's about time I share my secret pickled egg recipes with the rest of the world. You sure as hell ain't gonna find these in yer local general store, not these kind of eggs. You want good eggs, you gotta make em yerself. Now I know there are a lot of folks out there who don't know their way around a kitchen. Some folks can't even boil water. Keeping those people in mind, I have included two recipes: my "pickled eggs for dummies" recipe, and "T-Bone's Old Fashioned Pickled Eggs" recipe. Bon Appetit!

Pickled Eggs for Dummies

You will need:
1 good-sized jar of kosher dill pickles
8-10 eggs
1 can of jalapeno peppers (with carrot and onions if available)

Eat all the pickles and save that zesty pickle juice. Put yer eggs in a saucepan and cover em with water. Bring it to a boil and let it boil for about 10 minutes. Take the pan off the heat, cover it, and let it sit for a good 15 minutes. Pour cold water over the eggs until they are cool enough to handle. Now crack those babies carefully and peel the damn shells off, under running cold water of course. Be careful while yer peeling em, because you don't want em to get all hacked up or people will be afraid to eat em. Once they're all peeled, throw em in the pickle juice. Open the can of peppers and dump them in too, pepper juice and all. If you want em extra-spicy, put a little Tobasco sauce in there and maybe some black peppercorns. Now comes the tough part: put that lid on tight and leave em in the fridge for at least 2 weeks. Don't open the jar during that time. Shake them eggs up every day, so as to disperse the spices. Be patient, it takes time for a proper egg to brew. After 2 weeks goes by (or 3 if yer extra patient), open that jar and dig in. I like my eggs with some Tobasco and salt. Enjoy.

T-Bone's Old Fashioned Pickled Eggs

You will need:
5 cups of white wine vinegar
12 cloves of garlic
4 jalapeno peppers, sliced
4 tbsp of pickling spices (carried at yer local grocery store)
1 tsp of orange or lemon zest
2 cinnamon sticks, broken into thirds
12 hard-boiled eggs, peeled (follow the above recipe if you need to)
1 glass jar with a screw lid

Put all the ingredients (except the eggs) in a saucepan. Cover the pan and boil for about 10 minutes. Remove from heat and allow to cool. When cool, strain into the glass jar. Add the eggs and a few of the peppers, make sure they're all the way covered with the juice, and then screw that lid on tight. Put it yer fridge and let em age for 4-6 weeks, shaking em around every few days to mix the spices up good. Be patient.

HEROIC BREAKFASTS IN THE US OF A

BREAKFAST IS THE CORNERSTONE OF OUR DIETARY HEALTH. IT PROVIDES THE FUEL THAT KEEPS OUR BODIES IN MOTION. THEREFORE, IT IS NOT A MEAL TO BE TRIVIALIZED.

SEVERAL EATING ESTABLISHMENTS TAKE BREAKFAST QUITE SERIOUSLY (AS THEY SHOULD) SO SERIOUSLY IN FACT, THAT CERTAIN MENU ITEMS INVOKE IMAGES OF VIRILITY, COURAGE, & LUMBERJACKS! THESE ARE HEROIC BREAKFASTS...

It has been remarked, that Mickey's Dairy Bar in Madison, Wisc., features a five egg concoction with ham and cheese called *the Scrambler*. Square off the meal with one of their world famous malts for a true Dairyland feast.

The Palatine Inn of Palatine, Ill., salutes Greek mythology with their skillet sensation, *The Hercules*. Three eggs are accompanied by ham, hashbrowns, and a small glass of tomato juice. Mmmmm. Try fighting ten men after that!

Folks familiar with the Waffle House franchise won't soon forget the Southern gem on their menu. Hashbrowns take center stage as they get scattered, smothered, covered, chunked, topped, and diced. That's hashbrowns 6 different ways!

We have heard that the Country Kitchen in Cannon Falls, Minn., serves up a Midwest tour de force entitled, *the Barnbuster*. With four eggs, meat, and pancakes, some customers have been quoted as saying, "You betcha it's hard to get a clean plate after all that."

No nicknames are necessary for the omelets at Beth's Cafe in Seattle, Wash. Beth boasts a twelve egg omelet. God praise the man (or woman) that can eat a dozen eggs in one sitting - a true hero.

Letters

Dear Shovel Bum,
        I am an avid reader of your journal and have all the issues.
You're doing a great job and providing a terrific service to all of us
in the archaeology business. I'm writing because I need your advice.
Currently, I'm working as a crew chief on a large timber survey
project in northwestern Alabama. The problem is, my crew does not
respect me. Ever since the first day of the project, they've been
laughing at me, telling jokes about me behind my back, and even
throwing mud and slime on me. What can I do to regain their respect?
                                                    Bewildered in 'Bama

dear bewildered in 'bama,
        thanks for writing. it's good to hear from some of my loyal fans. your
problem is common, but also a very dangerous. the last thing you want as a
crew chief is a mutiny (see the excerpt from the new mexico field journal in the
current issue). regaining your crew's respect is not an easy thing, but it's
probably the most important thing you'll ever have to do. a surefire method
would be to single out a member of the crew and beat them into submission,
preferably in the crew's presence. you might consider using a mattock. with a
savage beating on everyone's mind, you'll be both respected and feared by
everyone. good luck!

Dear Shovel Bum,
        I'm interested in learning more about the evil robot-master, Dr. Krang. What's
his story?
                                                    Robot Lover

dear robot lover,
        take a look at dr. krang's origin story in issue two. keep your eyes
peeled — i'm sure the evil doctor will be back to plague shovel bum in future
issues.

Dear Shovel Bum,
        I work in the field at least 9 months of the year.
Let me tell you, I'm sick to death of eating beef jerky and
granola bars for lunch every day. What else would you
recommend for a more exciting field lunch?
                                                    Famished in the Field

dear famished in the field,
        you've come to the right person. there's no reason you should be limited
to jerky and granola in the field. sure, they're tasty and portable, but a diet
restricted to them leaves a lot to be desired. try a can of tuna, with crackers and
a miniature bottle of tobasco sauce. or how about a can of chili? it tastes just as
good straight from the can. some shovel bums i know prefer a lunch of canned
oysters served with sliced baguette or triscuits. others eat ramen noodles right
out of the bag, no water. believe it or not, they taste pretty good that way. and
have you ever considered eating a nice green apple?!!!

Chapter 3

LODGING

Like food, lodging also plays a big role in the shovel bum's field life. More often than not, field lodging is a sub-par motel, hence the "Motel Hell" issue of *Shovel Bum*. Most people have had at least one hellish motel experience, but I received several comments from people who wanted to contribute but had never had a bad experience. Maybe in the future we'll publish a "Motel Heaven" issue.

Motel Hell
By Jacqui Cheung

I wrote this description of our motel after about a two month long stay. We ended up staying there for about 5 months, which makes the situation even more hellish.

The Maple Cove Motel in Mountain Home, Idaho, is one of those long rectangular cinderblock units situated off the highway and painted brown and tan. The doors are orange, and ours (#6) has a splintery bullet hole just under the number. Ernie and Mary are the proprietors. They also run a diner which fronts the street. Ernie is friendly enough, a Pearl Harbor survivor according to his special license plate. He always seems eager to chat, which oddly enough makes me want to avoid him. His wife Mary is not pleasant, although I personally have never seen her act unpleasant. According to Guy and the maids, she is rather mean-spirited, suspicious and cheap. The maids get paid only $1.75 per room—so it's not the cleanest place and sometimes there is a lack of soap or towels.

The carpet is a dirty brown, and the seam has split under one of the beds, so the carpet looks bunched up and gaps to show the underlying decaying foam pad. There are two double beds. One mattress is distinctly concave—the one we sleep in is less so. Dark brown masonite panelling, dark brown coffee table between the beds, dark brown desk, dark brown chest of drawers stuck in a dark brown carpet-covered closet alcove. There is a picture of an elk glued to a board coated with glossy polyurethane. We have two brown ceramic lamps with yellowy shades and the light is very dim. It's like a cave. The bathroom is all right—fiberglass shower enclosure, newer linoleum. The toilet runs. Once we found a steak knife under the bed. The other couple on our crew came back from a break and found a pair of underwear in the cabinet under the sink.

The train tracks ran past our motel, and the trains were frequent. We had to turn on the air conditioner to drown out the train noises, and the sounds of the next room. For most of the summer, there seemed to be a car repair project in the parking lot.

 # Rogue Elk Inn
By Jacqui Cheung

It is December. She tells me on the phone "It's on the National Register... Zane Gray, and Teddy Roosevelt stayed there." I am suckered in. We arrive at night and see a large imposing wood frame inn, fronting the two lane highway. Broad stairs lead up to a wide porch lined with large posts supporting a second story balcony—a colonial revival style building built in the early part of the 20th century. This will be our home for 10 days, and after 10 days, we vow to never return. The inn probably relies on drop in visitors who arrive tired at night, not seeing beyond the facade. During daylight, the peeling paint, rotting foundation, and the moldering scatter of construction debris and fragments of plastic toys is evident. The innkeepers also have the adjacent diner, which specializes in smoked chicken—a dark dry stringy mass of meat in a dark sticky sauce.

"Improvements" have been made to the inn over the last few decades. The inn is cold. There are space heaters in the individual rooms, but we can see our breath in the common areas, and halls. Our room is fine, although minimally furnished, and our only heat from a circular electric heater, plugged into a dubious looking outlet. Our bathroom is down the hall and shared by other crew members. This bathroom was probably original to the house, but other bathrooms were added into closets. A bathroom was added into the room next door, the plumbing connecting up beneath the sink. They knocked a big hole in the wall, ran the pipes through it, and ran their electrical wire right next to the plumbing. A rag was stuffed in the hole, but I could still catch a glimpse of the adjacent bathroom. This method was used throughout.

About five of the male crew members shared a large room downstairs. A seventies style kitchen peninsula was added into it, but it looked incomplete, and unused for at least 10 years. The guys slept on cots across the floor and the room was heated with a large wood stove, which often went out. They shared a bathroom, which had hastily been installed in a small closet at the back of the main entrance hall. The fiberglass shower enclosure was just set into the space, not level, or attached to any framing and without a curtain. The back of the shower enclosure was visible from the entrance hall, and the enclosure didn't completely fill the opening, providing a view into the bathroom. There was always a puddle on the bathroom floor.

The kitchen was fitted with restaurant style sinks and appliances, some 10 to 15 years ago, and those items were probably in need of repair when installed. The large restaurant range was a rusting hulk with incomplete and broken parts. The working stove was a harvest gold electric one with 2 burners functioning out of 4. However, if the washing machine was in use in the next room, the stove did not function at all. In fact, the use of the washing machine seemed to overload most circuits and cause fuses to blow throughout the inn. The stainless steel sink sagged because it was missing a leg. We found a turned furniture post in a fireplace, and duct taped it in place under the sink to level it up. One day the kitchen got smoky when a crew member was cooking, and we found we couldn't open any windows. The window above the sink had a piece of cardboard taped over a big hole—it was probably broken out the last time the kitchen got smoky.

To make matters worse, the job was miserable—primarily standing in cold rain pushing clay through 1/8 inch mesh, and practically forbidden to talk. The main after work activity was to put on warm clothes, smoke, drink and play pool in a frigid downstairs room. Rumor has it that the place has since been closed down by the fire marshal.

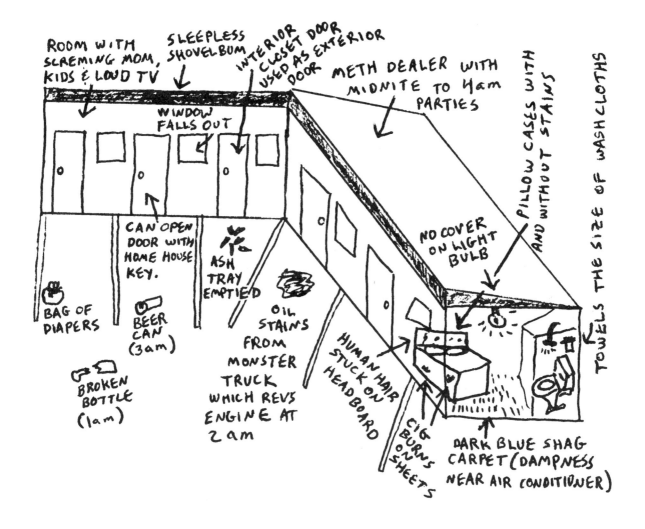

These rules were posted on the door at the Blue Spruce.

MOTEL RULES

1. WE HAVE A "ZERO TOLERANCE " AS FAR AS DRUGS ARE CONCERNED!!
NEXT, REGISTRATION: YOU MUST HAVE PROPER PICTURE I.D.! YOU CANNOT
RENT A ROOM FOR SOMEONE ELSE! IF YOU DO , THEY WILL BE EVICTED AND NO
REFUND WILL BE GIVEN, AND YOU WILL NOT BE ALLOWED TO RENT A ROOM
HERE AGAIN!
PETS ARE ALLOWED; BUT YOU MUST TELL US WHEN REGISTERING, AS THERE IS
A $15.00 DAILY CHARGE PER DAY. ALL PETS MUST BE ON A LEASH AND USE THE
DESIGNATED AREA FOR PETS, YOU WILL BE INFORMED WHEN REGISTERING
WHERE THAT IS. FAILURE TO TELL US WILL RESULT IN EVICTION WITHOUT
REFUND. NO CATS ALLOWED!!!
VISITORS;; ALL VISITORS MUST LEAVE BY 11;00 PM. THERE IS A $5.00 CHARGE
FOR A VISITOR SPENDING THE NIGHT AND THE OFFICE MUST BE NOTIFED
BEFORE 11;00 P.M. AND BE PAID THAT AMOUNT!!!
PARKING;; PARKING IS LIMITED TO ONE CAR PER ROOM , SO IF YOU HAVE MORE
THAN ONE VEHICLE , PLEASE CONTACT THE OFFICE FOR FUTHER INSTRUCTIONS
ON WHERE THEY MAY PARK!!
SNACK-SHACK IS OPEN FOR YOUR CONVENIENCE FROM 7:00 A.M. TO 10.00 P.M.!!
TELEPHONE::LOCAL CALLS ARE .25 CENTS A CALL. THERE IS NO CHARGE FOR
LONG-DISTANCE OR COLLECT CALLS (YOU MUST HAVE A CALLING CARD) OR
INCOMMING CALLS. PLEASE LIMIT YOUR CALLS TO 15 MINUTES A CALL SO
EVERYONE HAS ACCESS . ALSO PLEASE LIMIT YOUR INCOMMING CALLS . IF
YOU USE UP YOUR PHONE DEPOSIT, YOU MUST COME TO THE OFFICE DURING
OFFICE HOURSTO TURN YOUR PHONE BACK ON!!TO MAKE A LOCAL CALL,DIAL
9+NUMBER, LONG DISTANCE .FOLLOW YOUR INSTRUCTIONS ON YOUR CALLING
CARD. TO DIAL 800 NUMBER, DIAL9+1+800+NUMBER..
ANY ILLEGAL ACTIVITIES WILL BE REPORTED TO THE AUTHORITIES AND WILL
BE PROSECUTED!!! I.E. DRUGS, PROSTITUTION—ETC!!
HOUSEKEEKING:SERVICE IS PROVIDED DAILY!! HOUSEKEEPERS " MUST ENTER"
AND CLEAN ROOMS DAILY! IF YOU ARE STAYING MORE THAN ONE DAY, YOUR
TOWELS WILL BE COLLECTED AND REPLACED AND A LIGHT CLEANING WILL BE
DONE. IF YOU ARE STAYING ON A WEEKLY BASIS, YOU WILL RECEIVE CLEAN
TOWELS, LIGHT CLEANING , AND SHEETS WILL BE CHANGED TWICE A WEEK!!
WEEKLY RESIDENTS:: WEEKLY RESIDENTS WILL PAY THEIR WEEKLY RENT
PRIOR TO 11:00 A.M. ON THEIR CHECK- OUT DATE!!
CHECK-OUT IS 11:00 A.M. IF YOU WISH TO STAY ANOTHER DAY , YOU MUST
NOTIFY THE OFFICE AND PAY PRIOR TO 11:00 A.M.!!

THIS IS A FAMILY MOTEL AND WE WANT TO MAKE SURE YOUR STAY HERE IS
ENJOYABLE!! THAT IS WHY WE INSIST ON NO COMPANY AFTER 11:00 P.M. AND
NO TRAFFIC COMING AND GOING ALL NIGHT! AND NO LOUD PARTYING,AND
LOUD DISTURBANCES!! AS A PAYING CUSTOMER , YOU ARE ENTITLED TO A
GOOD-NIGHT'S REST!! IF YOU HAVE A PROBLEM NEIGHBOR AND WANT SOME
ASSISTANCE, PLEASE COME TO THE OFFICE AND RING THE BELL EVEN IF THE
CLOSED, WE WILL TAKE CARE OF THE PROBLEM IMMEDIATELY,

REMEMBER, IF WE DON"T KNOW THERE IS A PROBLEM, WE CAN:T HELP!!
FAILURE TO COMPLY WITH THESE RULES WILL RESULT IN EVICTION AND NO
REFUND WILL BE GIVEN!!!!!!
ANY DAMAGE OR EXPENSES WILL BE THE RESPONDSIBILTY OF PERSON(S)
REGISTERED FOR SAID ROOM(S)!!!!

SHOVEL BUM'S
Poetry Corner

The Shovelbum's Lot
Drunken night deskman
Scorns us while demanding that
we must buy him drinks

No cooking in rooms
we break this rule, yet mints still
left on the pillow

Bad porn on TV
Drinking alone in own's room
the shovelbum's lot
By Troy Lovata

The Blue Spruce Motel I
Sticky brown shag
Window falls out
No sleep tonight
By Cathy Bialas

The Blue Spruce Motel II
Forget your room key?
Your house key works as well
No security
By Trent DeBoer

Bull's Motel
They have kitchenettes
Bible turned to new page daily
KFC next door
By Betsy DeBoer

Castleberry's
Hundred plus heat index
Dripping air conditioner
Wet carpet underfoot
By Betsy DeBoer

Page 42 — Chapter 3

Letters

Dear Shovel Bum,

I once stayed in a motel that was built using the old city pool as its foundation. I swear that there was not a straight wall in the place; my room was like one of the 'optical illusion' rooms at the science museum or fair – one of those that makes a little fella look like a giant and vice versa. Anyway this place had two sections; a newer remodeled section and an older section. Naturally I went for the old cheap section (gotta save that per diem). The way I figure it the only thing between rooms was a couple of pieces of paneling so that you were basically living your neighbors lives as well as your own. Hopefully none of the ticks that constantly invaded my room everyday after work got thru to the other rooms – I wouldn't wish that terror on anyone (one guy on the crew used to take pleasure in leaving the ticks that he found on himself at restaurants while we were eating – places where unsuspecting children ran free – but I should save that story for another issue). The real problem here was the downstairs neighbor – I think. They certainly liked their fried food; don't get me wrong I too am a lover of all things fried – chicken, eggs, okra, pork chops, ice cream, french fried potatoes….. I think the vent from their room must have come out in my bathroom somewhere and when I left the door open when I went to work I would come home to a room that smelled like a fryer vat; and everything seemed to have a layer of grease on it. The worst part was that everything I had smelled like I worked in a kitchen hunkered over a deep fat fryer. I hated to go home after living there for ten days at a time smelling like I did; no one would believe that I was really an archaeologist. It was humiliating. Don't get me wrong; being a fry cook is a noble profession and I appreciate the fine job that they do. At least all my paperwork held up better in the rain.

Keep up the good work,

E. Arthur

Dear Shovel Bum:

I heard you were putting together an issue about interesting hotel experiences. Well, the following story doesn't involve a hotel, but your readers may find it interesting. I spent portions of two summers conducting surveys of a National Forest in Missouri. This would be the part where I should tell you about the hotel, but there was no hotel, because the project director was too cheap. He didn't even provide adequate camping equipment or a vehicle. We used a 1990 Ford Escort to travel the forest roads! You might be saying, 'you must have been rakin' in the per diem.' Nope, that wasn't provided either. The work was intense and the ticks, chiggers and powerful thunderstorms made things even more difficult. The only time the director spent in the field was part of one afternoon and he rented a car for himself to make the trip. You might think that the experience taught me a lesson. Wrong! I agreed to work for two more weeks the following summer. The accommodations were the same, BUT this time we received 5 whole dollars/day per diem. A generous sum based on the experience the summer before. This time the crew included the project director and the field conditions were even worse. The ticks were unbearable. There were days when we each picked off 20-40 ticks each. One crewmember even contracted Lyme's disease by the end of the project. This time we had an SUV, but the director would not allow us to make the 20-minute drive to civilization for anything. As I mentioned previously, we were sleeping in tents, which was fine most of the time. The director has an incredibly loud snoring habit. Frequently during the night, I would hear my friend unzip his tent and start throwing rocks at the director's tent until the snoring stopped. The silence would last 10-15 minutes before the snoring started again. My friend ran out of rocks nightly, so just before sunset each night he would gather up a fresh pile to arm himself for the night. That project has provided me with a lifetime's worth of stories. I'll send additional letters to shovel bum in the future.

Dazed and Malaised in Missouri

Chapter 4

VEHICLES

Field vehicles may be the most important piece of field equipment. It's not uncommon for these workhorses to haul six or more shovel bums and a full load of personal gear and field equipment up an unpaved, rutted mountain road under intense summer conditions. A good rig is hard to find and like a fine thoroughbred, truly deserves every shovel bum's reverence. Field vehicle repair is an invaluable trait of the shovel bum and should be prominently listed on every resume.

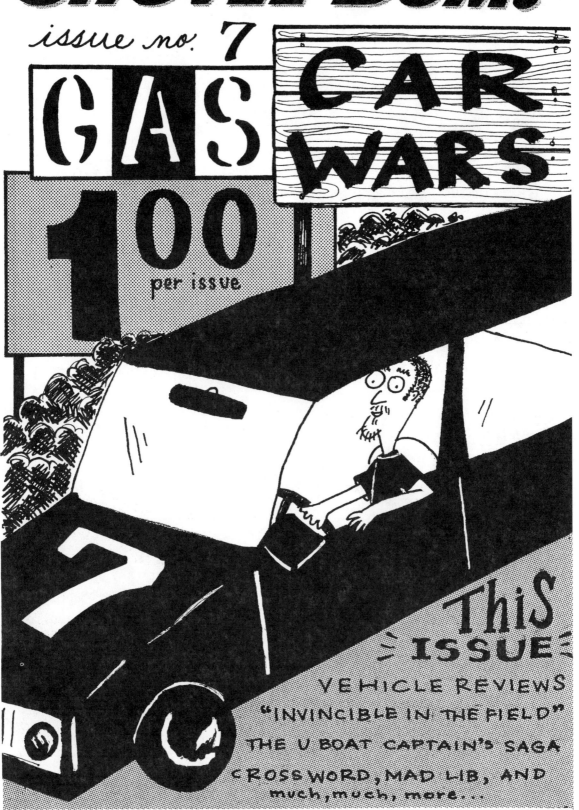

INVINCIBLE IN THE FIELD

...OR SO IT SEEMED, BECAUSE IT WAS A GAS SNORTIN', RUBBER BURNIN', TIRE SQUEALIN', CREW-CAB FORD!

351 CUBIC INCHES OF V-8

CATTLE PUSHER

FOUR DOORS, SEATS SIX!

TIPS THE SCALES AT OVER 3 TONS!

MUD BOGGIN' TIRES!

BY "DOC" TROY FALL '01

THANK THE ABSURDLY LOW GAS PRICES OF THE '90'S.

CHEAPER THAN BOTTLED WATER!

TEXAS CRUDE

NINE MILES PER GALLON RATING BE DAMNED.

YOU'D HARDLY KNOW WE'RE CROSSING A CORNFIELD AT 70 MILES PER HOUR!

THE IGLOO COOLER RAN OFF THE TRUCK'S CIGARETTE LIGHTER.

IT SEEMED PERFECT FOR THE SOUTH TEXAS HEAT!

A SIMPLE X-MAS GIFT WOULD BRING DOWN THIS MIGHTY VEHICLE.

GEE...THE DOME LIGHT DOESN'T SEEM TO BE WORKING...

UNTIL WE RAN DOWN THE TRUCK'S BATTERY.

"JUST TRYING TO HELP"
by Geof Prairie

IT WAS A CRISP FALL DAY IN WEST CENTRAL WISCONSIN

I WAS DRIVING OUR CREW'S JEEP CHEROKEE THROUGH THE BACK ROADS OF THE ARMY BASE WHERE WE WORKED

WE'D LEFT SOME EQUIPMENT BACK AT HEADQUARTERS. I VOLUNTEERED TO DRIVE BACK AND PICK IT UP.

I WASN'T REALLY SUPPOSED TO BE DRIVING.

THE ARMY MADE YOU DO SOME TRAINING BEFORE YOU COULD USE THEIR VEHICLES. A WEEK BEFORE, ON A SLOW DAY, I SIGNED UP.

THE BOSS WASN'T HAPPY ABOUT THIS — I'D SIGNED UP WITHOUT ASKING. BUT HE DIDN'T SAY I COULDN'T DRIVE THE JEEP.

I'D FIGURED THAT IT'D MAKE ME WORTH MORE AS AN EMPLOYEE. I WAS THE ONLY ONE ON OUR CREW WITHOUT ANY EXPERIENCE IN ARCHEOLOGY. I WAS TIRED OF BEING THE LOW MAN ON THE TOTEM POLE.

I TOOK A LEFT, AND A WATER JUG IN THE BACK TIPPED OVER.

I KNEW THE JUG WOULD LEAK IF LEFT ON ITS SIDE, SO I LEANED OVER TO PICK IT UP. I HELD ON TIGHT TO THE STEERING WHEEL...

AND DROVE THE JEEP OVER THE EDGE OF AN EMBANKMENT.

IT ALL HAPPENED IN SLOW MOTION.
(I WAS ONLY GOING AROUND 10 MPH)
THE SEAT BELT HELD ME IN—I WASN'T EVEN
SCRATCHED. BUT I TOTALED THE JEEP.

IT WAS TRICKY TO FIGURE OUT HOW TO
UNDO MYSELF. I HAD TO ROLL DOWN
A SIDE WINDOW TO CRAWL OUT

I CLIMBED BACK UP TO THE ROAD
AND WAVED DOWN A DUMPTRUCK

ALL RIGHT THERE. TAKE IT EASY, SON

THE DRIVER GOT OUT AND STARTED
SHAKING ME, TRYING TO GET ME
TO CALM DOWN. I WAS REALLY
RATTLED—I'D GONE PALE.

Y'KNOW, WHEN I FIRST GOT THIS TRUCK, I ROLLED IT OVER ON THE SECOND DAY.

AS WE DROVE BACK TO PICK UP
THE REST OF MY CREW, HE
KEPT CHATTING WITH ME.

I COULDN'T HELP BUT THINK IT'D
BE PRETTY COOL TO SHOW UP IN
A DUMPTRUCK, OTHERWISE.

WE CRAMMED INTO THE CAB. I SAT ON THE FLOOR AND OUR SUPER-VISOR HAD TO HOLD ON OUTSIDE. WE DROVE SLOWLY BACK TO HEADQUARTERS.

NOBODY SAID ANYTHING ELSE FOR THE REST OF THE RIDE.

SHOVEL BUM VEHICLE REVIEWS

Picking the right field vehicle can be a harrowing task. Pick the wrong one and you risk inefficiency, humiliation, and a fiery death. But how to pick the right vehicle? The internet? Bah, you'll only find corporate hoo haw and bald-faced lies. How about *Consumer Reports*? Sure, if you've hours to waste wading through page after page of boring statistics and technical jargon. What you need is a straightforward, shoot-from-the-hip review of the latest and greatest from the Motor City. You need the Shovel Bum Vehicle Review.

The following reviews are drawn from three field seasons at the Yakima Training Center—the worst vehicle conditions this side of northern Mongolia. YTC is a land of extreme temperatures, with numerous creek crossings, boulders everywhere, and military shrapnel glittering like jewels in every road. The good roads are graveled—with gravel the size of musk melons—and the bad roads still give me nightmares.

Let us first examine the **Ford Explorer**. Surprisingly (considering all the bad press the Explorer received this year), the Explorer did pretty good at the YTC. Sure, the clearance is bad and we bottomed out in most every creek crossing, but the good old *Exploder* (as we affectionately dubbed it; AKA the *Moon Buggy*) made it through all three seasons with the same engine, bumper, and major parts. However, we did have to replace a ruptured radiator, upgrade to 10-ply tires, and invest $1400 in replacing the 4WD wiring (which had melted during one of the semi-regular undercarriage brush fires; see Figure 1).

- *The Pros*: CD player, widely available parts, somewhat roomy
- *The Cons*: no skid plate, loose handling (moon buggy), bad tires

Figure 1. Expensive Rewiring Job
at the Dealership.

Next we turn to the **Ford F-150** King-Cab pickup. Now here is a real field vehicle. Good clearance, true power, roomy interior, and lots of storage capacity. No CD player, but is that really necessary? Plus, the bench seats can't compare to bucket seats with balloon lumbar support. Unfortunately, I only saw the F-150 in action for 20 field days, so I'm not sure how it would hold out over the long haul.

- *The Pros*: clearance, power, storage capacity
- *The Cons*: comfort, too long, no CD player

And now for a surprise—the **Chevy Safari** Mini-Van! Please don't ask me why this vehicle was brought to the YTC, suffice it to say that it only lasted two days. It took one marginally deep creek crossing for the Safari to show its true colors. But talk about spacious comfort (see Figure 2)!

- *The Pros*: smooth ride, cushy seats, nice upholstery
- *The Cons*: zero clearance, no power, no 4WD

Figure 2. Spacious Enough for Several Standing Screens.

While we Americans are so very proud of our SUVs and our monster trucks, the Japanese have quietly been manufacturing their own brand of efficient and reliable field vehicles. The **Mitsubishi Montero** Sport made two appearances at the YTC. The first Montero worked out pretty well—until we drove through a deep creek and shorted out the entire electrical system. It was not much fun driving home on the freeway with the Montero stuck in 4WL. The next one lasted through the end of the season with no real problems to speak of.

- *The Pros*: power, good handling, short vehicle length
- *The Cons*: cramped, not good in water, street tires

Then there was the **Dodge Durango**. Like the Explorer, this vehicle kept on going and going. Then we heard from the rental company that the engine burned up a week after we turned it in. Still, while we had it, it was great—lots of room (three rows of seats), CD player <u>and</u> cassette, good air conditioning, etc. One word of warning: be sure and specify that you want 4WD. We made the mistake of renting another Durango and found out the hard way that 4WD is not standard.

- *The Pros*: power, smooth ride, roomy
- *The Cons*: street tires, back seats are uncomfortable

If you're looking for a top of the line field vehicle, get yerself a **Chevy Tahoe**. This behemoth took to the YTC like a penguin takes to water. The ride was smooth even on the roughest of roads and the roominess made even the lowliest crew members feel like kings. But as they say, the bigger they are, the harder they fall. On its first day in the field, the Tahoe suffered from two simultaneous flat tires (see Figure 3). We ended up having to leave it in the field over night and had to shuttle people out with another vehicle.

- *The Pros*: mighty power, smoothest of rides, monstrously roomy
- *The Cons*: weak tires, only two rows of seats

Figure 3. Learn to Change Tires Like the Pit Crews!

A field vehicle review column would not be complete without the **Jeep Grand Cherokee**. This long-time favorite performed adequately at the YTC, if only for an abbreviated tour of duty. For its size, the Grand Cherokee was quite powerful and handled well. But like the Montero, it's a little too small for hauling crew around. And much to our chagrin, the spare tire is not standard in size! We certainly did not enjoy driving the Grand Cherokee down shrapnel-encrusted YTC roads with a little donut tire.

- *The Pros*: power, handling, short vehicle length, comfortable seats
- *The Cons*: weak tires, cramped, tiny spare tire

GENERALLY BAD FIELD VEHICLE DECISIONS I HAVE WITNESSED...

by Geof Prairie

Seattle Police Blotter

Wedgwood/6:30 A.M./3900 Block 115th Street/Vandalism
Officer Swenson responds to a vandalism call in the posh
Wedgwood district of Seattle. Upon arriving on the scene, a Mr.
California Doo Rag, aka California Coop, approached the officer
directing her attention to a scratched word on the side of his 1999
Toyota Tacoma pick-up truck. "R E D N E C K" had been crudely
scratched into the panel behind the driver's side door beneath the
extended cab's wing window overnight. The officer noted a Shovel
Bum shield decal that was affixed to the inside of the wing window
as the likely cause for the seemingly random act of vandalism.
Photographs were taken, fingerprints were ignored and the crime
went unsolved.

Letters

MY RUNAWAY F250

Many people are born into families with generations of brand loyalty to a particular make of automobile. For example, I recently saw a brand new Ford 4 x 4 pickup with the huge tires and a lift kit that gave it about four feet of ground clearance. As I pulled up behind this truck at a stop light, I was looking eye-level at a bumper sticker that read "Bite me Chevy boy!"

One fellow I know has a saying that he would rather be sitting in a dead Chevy than seen in any Ford running or otherwise. And of course who hasn't heard the old saying "Ford" stands for fix or repair daily?

My parents owned mostly Chevrolets. Over the years there were a couple Pontiacs and an Olds but they never strayed far from the world of General Motors products. For the most part, I have maintained this tradition in the countless old war-horses that I have owned. But my field vehicle horror story involves the *only* Ford that I have ever owned—a ¾-ton '87 Ford pickup.

This vehicle incident happened early one freezing October morning in Rexford, Montana. I was driving and Randy Pierre was riding shotgun. The truck was still very cold and in a high idle when we parked it to grab a cup of coffee at a Stop'n Go. I left the motor running with the gear selector in "park." We were nearly through the front door of the store when out of the corner of my eye I saw the truck moving in reverse. Because it was idling high and moving down hill, it was rapidly gaining speed and headed toward a set of gas pumps. I ran behind the truck to get to the driver side, opened the door, managed to get my right leg just far enough inside to stomp on the brake. As I was hitting the brake, I fell back out of the truck and rolled under the door as the truck slammed into two steel posts that were between the gas pumps. I had pulled the steering wheel as I fell out of the truck causing it to miss the gas pumps altogether.

Aside from my scrapes and bruises, I was miraculously unscathed and there was no significant damage to the gas station equipment. The truck was (and still is) another story. After some shade-tree body work in Montana, it is now known as the 4-tone.

There are those individuals who believe that I never really had the gear selector in Park. But as far as I am concerned I did and the way I see it, my first Ford nearly killed me. So I guess I will be taking this brand loyalty thing a bit more seriously. And of course I have started using the parking brake—our new Field Safety Rule #1.

Randall Schalk

Chapter 5

TOLT

Tolt, Trent de Boer
Creek Baseball at Tolt Field, California Doo-Rag
Cover art: Betsy de Boer

Every once in a while, a huge data recovery project comes along and snaps up every working shovel bum in the region. In the fall of 1998, the Tolt data recovery project in King County, Washington, gave steady employment to every shovel bum from Seattle to Portland. I stumbled onto this project immediately upon moving to Washington State and subsequently was introduced to the Northwest's finest shovel bums. There's nothing quite like working back-to-back 10-day sessions for several months with 30+ archaeologists—it's an experience that only shovel bums can relate to.

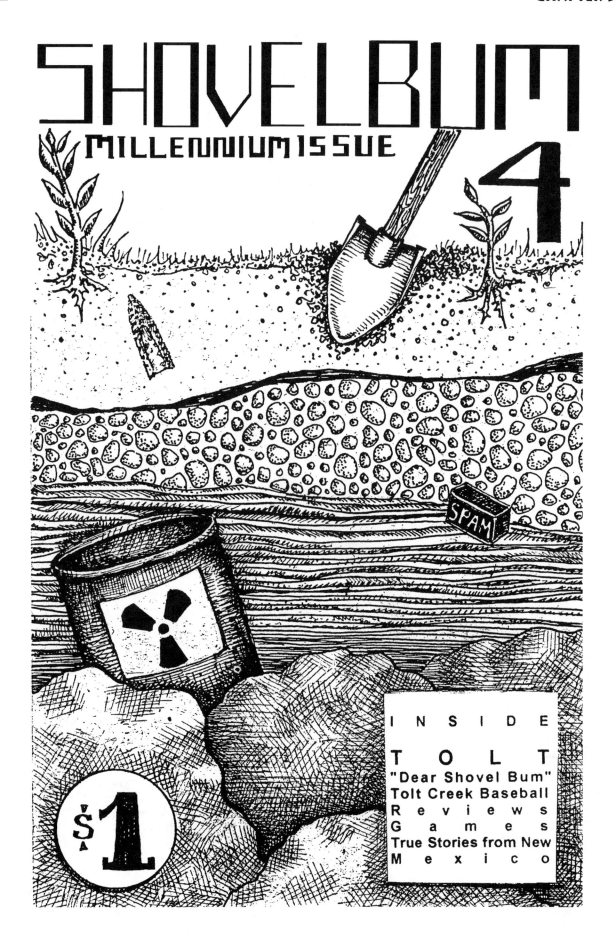

PEOPLE WHO HAVE READ SHOVEL BUM BEFORE HAVE PROBABLY FIGURED OUT THAT I'M SORT OF OBSESSED WITH OLD-STYLE 50'S ROBOTS.

AFTER A FEW WEEKS OF DIGGING AT TOLT, I EVEN STARTED ACTING LIKE A ROBOT. I WAS VERY EFFICIENT IN THE WAY I EXCAVATED AND FILLED OUT MY EXCAVATION LEVEL FORMS.

MY X-RAY VISION WILL HELP ME FIND ARTIFACTS

PART OF THE NICKNAME CAME FROM THE UNEARTHLY SPEED AT WHICH I EXCAVATED. YET I WAS VERY PRECISE.

YOU ALL RIGHT DOWN THERE T-BONE?

ALMOST DONE BOSS.

I THINK EVERY ARCHAEOLOGIST HAS FANTASIZED ABOUT A ROBOT DIGGING MACHINE. IT'S A COMMON TOPIC OF CONVERSATION AT BIG DATA RECOVERY PROJECTS.

I'D HAVE MY ROBOT DIG WITH A VACUUM ATTACHMENT.

OH, LIKE A FLOW-VEE

SOON I EARNED THE NICKNAME DIGBOT 6000, NAMED AFTER THE POWERFUL PIMPBOT 5000 ON THE CONAN O'BRIEN SHOW.

MY ERSTWHILE PARTNER ED AND I WERE IN AN UNSPOKEN COMPETITION FOR THE TITLE OF FASTEST EXCAVATOR WEST OF THE MIGHTY MISSISSIPPI.

WHAT LEVEL T-BONE?

LEVEL 9, YOU?

THE COMPANY RUNNING THE TOLT PROJECT WAS CALLED BOAS. IT'S OWNED AND RUN BY ASTRIDA BLUKAS-ONAT. HER WIENER DOG DELPHIE ANNOUNCED HER ARRIVAL AT THE SITE EACH DAY.

WE HAD SEVERAL FIELD DOGS OUT THERE EVERY DAY. OUR FAVORITE DOG WAS NAMED CODY, BUT WE QUICKLY RENAMED HIM QUAKO. HE WAS THE BEST STICK DOG ANY OF US HAD SEEN.

HE WOULD CHASE STICKS ALL DAY LONG, UNTIL HIS JOINTS WERE FINALLY STOVE UP. THEN HIS MA CATHY WOULD GET MAD AT US AND TAKE HIM AWAY.

ONE OF QUAKO'S BEST DAYS AT TOLT HAD TO BE THE 2ND WIENER FRENZY. THE WIENER FRENZY CONCEPT WAS ONE OF MY BRAINCHILDREN → COMPLETE CHAOS WITH GRILLED HOT DOGS AND BRATWURST. IT WAS GREAT.

NO ONE KNOWS EXACTLY HOW MANY HOT DOGS QUAKO ATE DURING THE 2ND WIENER FRENZY, BUT IT WAS WAY MORE THAN A DOG OF HIS SIZE SHOULD HAVE BEEN ABLE TO EAT.

QUAKO EVENTUALLY PUKED ALL HIS HOT DOGS UP AND SPENT THE DAY LAYING ON HIS SIDE, PANTING. HE DID TRY TO EAT THE HOT DOGS AGAIN LATER, BUT MOST OF US TRIED TO STOP HIM.

ONE DAY, A BUNCH OF FOLKS NOTICED WHAT THEY THOUGHT WAS A FRESH COUGAR TRACK RIGHT NEAR THE SITE.

THIS WAS RIGHT AROUND ONE OF THE TIMES I WAS PLANNING ON CAMPING OUT AT THE SITE WITH MY CO-WORKERS CALIFORNIA DOO-RAG AND McSWILLUP.

WE HAD A GREAT CAMP SET UP ON A TERRACE BELOW THE SITE. ON A CLEAR NIGHT, WE'D SLEEP OUT UNDER THE STARS, WITH MOSS FOR A PILLOW.

McSWILLUP THOUGHT AHEAD AND BROUGHT HIS FULLY-LOADED RED RIDER BB GUN. WE SET UP A SHOOTING RANGE THAT NIGHT AND BACKLIT THE TARGETS WITH OUR FLASHLIGHTS.

ONE OF THE TARGETS WAS AN UNCOOKED HOT DOG STICKING OUT OF A BEER BOTTLE. I NAILED IT ON MY FIRST ATTEMPT, IMPRESSING EVERYONE.

THE ONLY PROBLEM WAS WE COULDN'T FIND THE HOT DOG. EITHER IT WAS DISINTEGRATED FROM MY SHOT, OR SOME FOREST CREATURE GOT IT. I DREAMT THE COUGAR SMELLED IT, CAME BACK FOR MORE, AND FOUND ME SLEEPING.

I LIVED THROUGH THAT NIGHT, BUT IT WAS ONE OF THE LAST NICE NIGHTS WE HAD. THERE WAS ONE OTHER NIGHT → A HUGE FEAST WE ALL ATTENDED.

I'M GRILLING THE SALMON IN THE TRADITIONAL SNOQUALMIE WAY

AFTER THAT FEAST, IT STARTED RAINING AND NEVER REALLY STOPPED. WE BUILT RAIN SHELTERS TO MAKE OUR WORK EASIER.

BUT YOU STILL HAD TO GO OUTSIDE IN THE RAIN TO SCREEN AT THE BLOCK WHERE I WORKED. IT WAS WET AND COLD.

TO SURVIVE IN THESE CONDITIONS, I INGESTED A DAILY DOSE OF COFFEE AND GOGURT → THE YOGURT FOR THOSE ON THE GO!

MMMM, BLUE!

EAGLE-EYE USED HIS LUNCH BREAKS TO HUNT THE NEWTS THAT BECAME TRAPPED IN OUR COMPLETED EXCAVATION BLOCKS. THEY CAME OUT IN DROVES WHEN IT RAINED.

ONE MORNING WE FOUND A MOUNTAIN BEAVER HAD FALLEN INTO AN EXCAVATION BLOCK. IT WAS LIKE CATCHING A GREASED HOG TRYING TO GET HIM OUT.

GET HIM T-BONE!

ANIMALS PLAYED A PRETTY BIG ROLE AT THE TOLT SITE. OUR MASCOT WAS A TREE ROOT THAT LOOKED LIKE ONE OF THOSE STUFFED SOCK MONKEYS.

OUR MONKEY MASCOT WAS NOT TO BE CONFUSED WITH THE HELPER MONKEYS WHO STARTED VISITING THE SITE TOWARDS THE END OF THE PROJECT. WE GAVE TOURS OF THE SITE TO LOCAL SCHOOL CHILDREN, WHO WERE AFFECTIONATELY CALLED HELPER MONKEYS BY SOME OF THE CREW.

WE ALSO HAD A LOT OF MEDIA OUT THERE. IT WAS HARD TO EXCAVATE WITH A CAMERA AND MICROPHONE IN YOUR FACE.

WE ALL GAVE THE NEWS PEOPLE THE SAME NAME...

WE SURE DID FIND SOME COOL ARTIFACTS AT THE TOLT SITE.

AT THE END OF THE PROJECT, WE ALL WENT OUR SEPARATE WAYS, KNOWING WE WOULD WORK TOGETHER SOON.

Creek Baseball at Tolt Field by California Doo-Rag

Originally played a few years ago along the Washington coast near the Ozette River, Creek Baseball reached a new level of professionalism during the recent archaeological excavations at Stuwe'yuq near the Tolt River in eastern King County.

Creek Baseball is a hybrid game comprised from baseball, Over-The-Line (OTL), stick ball, and Wiffle ball. Creek Baseball is a competitive sport played by both sexes and by all ages. Rules adhere to the basic laws of baseball (e.g., three strikes equal an out, three outs in a half inning, nine inning games, and with each player taking a turn at bat each inning). Equipment for Creek Baseball involves handcrafted bats fastened from locally available timber and semi-rounded to rounded cobbles larger than a quarter and small enough that they do not break the bat. The game is played by the pitcher, who is positioned 1.5 to 2 meters away from the batter, lobbing the rounded cobble into the strike zone aiming its trajectory so that it lands on home plate if the batter does not swing. The batter swings his/her bat through the strike zone trying to put the rounded cobble into play. A player is considered out if they make contact with the rounded cobble and it does not clear the automatic out zone. Singles, doubles, triples, and home runs move ghost base runners around the figurative diamond according to the type of hit. Runners are always forced. In-field fly rule is always in effect with less than two out.

Tolt Field, located in a clear-cut which was once a mixed deciduous and coniferous forest, was a classic field with irregular dimensions and a story underneath every rock (Figure 1). Right field was a short porch only 75 feet away from home plate. It took a Herculean hit of 250 feet to clear the left and center field fence and it happened more than once. A stump located between the single and double demarcation points had a monkey placed on top of it. It was to be an automatic grand slam if the batter was able to hit the monkey on the fly with a batted rounded cobble. It never happened. It was just one of those crazy items that made Tolt Field unique.

Two of the games greatest, McSwillop and California Doo-Rag (CDR), played Creek Baseball relentlessly at Tolt Field during the 1998 field season. At lunch time, as the rest of the crew rested their weary bones from excavating, McSwillop and CDR elevated the game of Creek Baseball from a backwater hick pastime to a national phenomenon. Powered by the love of the game and THC, McSwillop and CDR revolutionized Creek Baseball with their innovative bat designs. Amassing huge numbers during the season, McSwillop ended the year with 45 home runs, 200 runs batted in, and a batting average above .400. Searching for the right piece of timber for a bat became an obsession of CDR and eventually led to his untimely fall down a steep hill at Tolt during the rainy season. He is currently on the inactive roster and is expected to return during Spring Training. McSwillop went to Cuba during the off season and played winter Creek Baseball with some of the brightest stars of tomorrow.

If you would like to learn more about Creek Baseball, email me at <cooperjb9@netscape.net>

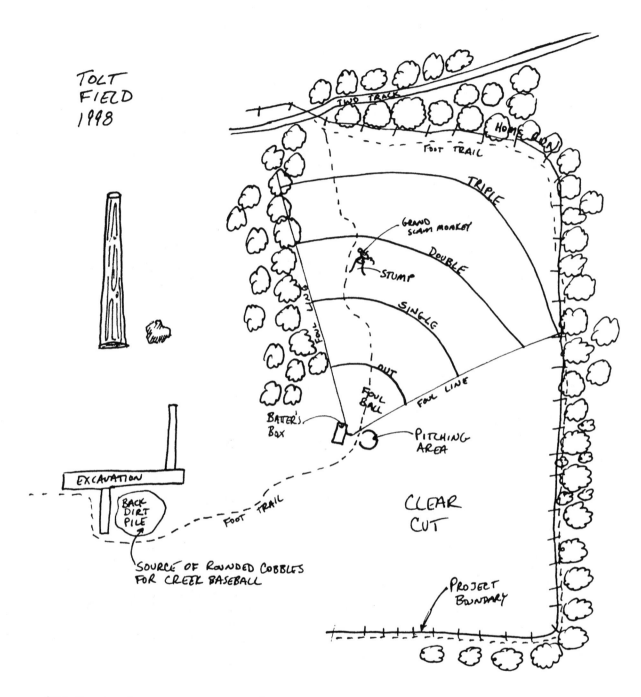

TOLT
FIELD
1998

FIGURE 1.

Chapter 6

MILITARY WORK

YTC, Trent de Boer
Shovel Bum Meets the Bomb Squad, Geof Prairie
Bomb Scare, Abner R.
Firecracker, Abner R.
Cover art: Betsy de Boer

Indirectly, the Department of Defense is one of the biggest employers of shovel bums in the country. Thanks to Section 110 of the National Historic Preservation Act, Federal installations must be inventoried for cultural resources. Military installations can be huge places and these projects have been real cash cows for a lot of CRM companies. It's kind of ironic when the more left-leaning shovel bums work at military installations—it's a potential recipe for disaster that couldn't be more perfect for the pages of *Shovel Bum!*

USUALLY THE DIRT ROADS AT YTC MAKE FOR SMOOTH SAILING. BUT WHEN IT RAINS, LOOK OUT!

SLOW MOVING TANK CARAVANS ARE THE WORST.

ONE MORNING WE WERE STOPPED BY A SQUAD OF CANADIAN SOLDIERS WHO WERE INVOLVED IN WAR GAMES. THEY WERE VERY SUSPICIOUS.

ANOTHER TIME WE WERE "ESCORTED" OFF BASE BY MP'S DUE TO A COMM. SNAFU.

THE WAR ON TERRORISM AND THE IRAQ WAR MADE SCHEDULING A NIGHTMARE.

THE ARMY HAS STARTED CLOSING ROADS IN SOME ENVIRONMENTALLY SENSITIVE AREAS.

ACCESS TO AREAS NEAR THE CENTRAL IMPACT ZONE ARE ESPECIALLY RESTRICTED THEY CALL THIS AREA THE "SAFETY DANGER ZONE".

IT IS PRETTY NERVE WRACKING TO WORK NEAR ACTIVE TRAINING MANEUVERS.

FOR ALL THE HASSLES, IT'S HARD NOT TO BE AFFECTED BY THE HARSH BEAUTY OF THE SAGEBRUSH STEPPE.

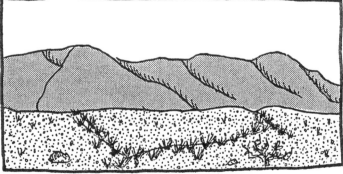

WE EVEN FOUND OFFICER TRAINING MANUALS WITH INSTRUCTIONS ON HOW TO TREAT PRISONERS OF WAR!

ONE DAY WE FOUND A CASE OF MREs. WE HAD A MRE POTLUCK THE NEXT DAY.

THEY CALL THIS GRILLED BEEFSTEAK?!

EVEN IF SOME OF THEM TASTE BAD, THE COOKING TECHNOLOGY IS STILL OFF THE HOOK!

YOU CAN COOK THEM WITH YER OWN URINE!

SINCE YTC RANGE CONTROL MADE US CHECK IN/OUT IN PERSON EACH DAY, WE NOW STAY IN YAKIMA INSTEAD OF ELLENSBURG.

TONIGHT WE DINE AT EL RANCHITO!

OLÉ!

WE ALWAYS GO TO BERT GRANT'S ON TIGHTWAD TUESDAYS.

SALUD!

AS ALWAYS, BOWLING PLAYS A BIG ROLE IN OUR FIELD LIVES.

RODEO BOWL

COME ON TURKEY!

ONE YEAR, WE HELD ELABORATE TROPHY CEREMONIES AFTER EACH GAME.

GOOD GAME

THE BOWLING SCORES OF SEVERAL SEASONS ARE CURATED BY DUCK.

A LOT OF GREAT PEOPLE HAVE WORKED WITH ME AT YTC.

I WISH I COULD INCLUDE THEM ALL

THERE ARE STILL MANY ACRES LEFT TO SURVEY AT YTC, SO STAY TUNED!

LATER!

SHOVEL BUM meets the B💣MB SQUAD!

-OR- HOW I LEARNED TO STOP WORRYING AND LOVE UNEXPLODED ORDNANCE

SURVEY WORK, FORT McCOY, WISCONSIN

FT. McCOY WAS A US ARMY RESERVE BASE.

A LARGE SECTION OF THE LAND WAS SET ASIDE AS THE RECEIVING END OF HEAVY MUNITIONS TRAINING. THIS AREA, FULL OF TOXINS AND UNEXPLODED MISFIRES, WAS ABSOLUTELY **OFF-LIMITS.**

WE WERE WORKING RIGHT NEXT TO IT.

OUR SITE

STAY OUT OF HERE!

WE WERE USED TO FEELING THE GROUND TREMBLE AS THEY FIRED THE BIG GUNS

AND WE'D FIND LOTS OF INTERESTING STUFF, LIKE THIS BELT OF BLANKS FOR A MACHINE GUN.

LOOKS LIKE I'M ALL SET FOR HALLOWEEN.

BUT THIS WAS A **BIG** SHELL. WE WONDERED IF THERE MIGHT BE MORE LYING AROUND, SO WE CALLED IN TO HQ. THEY SENT OUT THE BOMB TECHS.

THEY QUICKLY DECIDED THAT IT WAS HARMLESS, BUT WORTH BLOWING UP ANYWAY, SO THEY TOOK IT OUT TO AN EMPTY FIELD AND RIGGED IT UP. WE WEREN'T INVITED TO WATCH.

BOOM!

I WAS A LITTLE DISAPPOINTED. I'D IMAGINED A SCENE WITH MORE DRAMA...

<TIC>
<TIC>
<TIC>

SOON AFTER THAT, WE WENT TO ORDNANCE TRAINING. WE WERE SHOWN THE VARIETY OF GRENADES, SHELLS, AND SO ON THAT WE MIGHT FIND IN THE FIELD. IT WAS COMPLETELY USELESS. THERE WAS **WAY** TOO MUCH STUFF TO REMEMBER.

THERE WERE ONLY TWO THINGS I REMEMBERED: THE BOMB-HANDLING **ROBOT** ON DISPLAY (SADLY, NOT FUNCTIONAL) AND A CABINET FULL OF EXPLOSIVES (HAPPILY, ALSO NOT FUNCTIONAL) TUMBLING TO THE FLOOR.

AAAH!

AFTER A FEW HOURS, WE RESOLVED THAT IF WE FOUND ANYTHING ELSE, WE'D REPORT IT, AND LEFT IT AT THAT. THERE WAS ONE FINAL PIECE OF ADVICE:

WHAT WOULD HAPPEN IF WE WERE TO HIT ONE OF THESE THINGS WITH A SHOVEL?

TRY NOT TO DO THAT.

OH, WELL. AT LEAST WE'D BEEN ISSUED STEEL-TOED BOOTS.

IT'S ALL THEY COULD FIND.

GEOF ALWAYS DID HAVE SUCH NICE TOENAILS.

AND HERE'S A TIP FOR THE FORT McCOY BOMB SQUAD: IF THAT ROBOT IS STILL NOT WORKING, DON'T SWEAT IT. HELP IS ON THE WAY.

MOROCCO OFFERS U.S. MONKEYS TO DETONATE MINES

RABAT, D.C., Morocco, March 24 (UPI) — A Moroccan publication accused the government Monday of providing unusual assistance to US troops fighting in Iraq by offering them 2000 monkeys trained in detonating land mines.

The weekly al-Usbu' al-Siyassi reported that Morocco offered the US forces a large number of monkeys, some from Morocco's Atlas Mountains and others imported, to use them for detonating land mines planted by the Iraqis.

Geof Prairie '03

Bomb Scare

I'm not saying my memories are any more valid or correct than Prairie's, just different. Prairie remembers a robot defusing the shell. I remember a robot as well, but my robot was a non-functioning

Must defuse bomb . . .
Must defuse bomb . . .

Prairie
ca. 1994

prototype in storage at Fort McCoy's Ordinance Disposal Office; they did have a working robot, but it was stationed at some airport in Chicago or Minneapolis. J.J. has her own memories of the event.

She says Prairie, T-Bone, and I were poking at the shell with our shovels; I know that's not true.

Oops!

When the Ordinance Disposal guys gave us a presentation on unexploded bombs, they showed us the robot, sitting there quietly in the corner, its little arm made from Erector Set parts, its little camera eyeball dark and dead. The sergeant in charge of the presentation reached into a cabinet full of dummy grenades and mortars to show us one he felt was especially interesting or educational. As he pulled it out, he knocked over a grenade which caused the rest to domino and spill out of the cabinet. Panicking, I

Wow! This is a great idea!

You're not so tough!

Oh god! No! Stop!

CLANK!

dove under the table, to everyone's delight. If anyone hit the shell with their shovels, I wasn't involved, I was probably running back to the Jeep.

My most vivid memories of the bomb actually have nothing to do with the bomb. I remember a tree-- the biggest tree I've seen at McCoy, probably

2 m in diameter-- with a hole in it where a shell had been shot through it. The tree was dying. I remember the ordnance guy hopping out of his truck and urinating against a tire right in front of us.

The bomb boys lugged the shell out of the woods on their shoulders. When one guy got tired, he simply tossed the shell on the ground, tip up, and let the other guy pick it up. We went back to our survey transects. An hour or so later we heard a thump! as the wired shell blew

up in a ditch across the road.

I'll make a deal with Prairie; if he includes the peeing soldier in his version of the story, I'll include the robot in mine. It's a nice touch, I'll admit. Hell, we can both throw in J.J.'s fable about hitting the shell with shovels. Only this time, I'll give it a good whack.

Abner R.

Shit . . .

Firecracker

After Ft. McCoy, I worked at a number of Army bases, but the most memorable soldier I ever encountered was while working at an excavation in the Badlands in 1996, which is unquestionably the most beautiful place on earth.
He was called 'Parachute Dan' because he

slept under a parachute draped over his truck. He had spent the better part of the last decade in the Marines, and this was his first experience out of the military.
On the Fourth of July a short thunderstorm rolled across the Plains and a local man in a

small truck sped into camp, telling us there was a grass fire over the hill. We threw shovels into the back of our trucks and raced to the fire; I was excited because I'd never fought a fire before. However, by the time we made it there, the rain picked up and it was clear that the fire would be out in a few minutes.

We were watching the rain do its job when over the hill came Dan, sprinting through the gale, wearing only shorts, a shirt and flip-flops. He stopped when he made it to the fire, stunned that he had nothing to fight the fire with. He pulled off his t-shirt, and started wacking the smoldering grass with it. We honked, and shouted, but he was too far away to hear us. At first we laughed and poked fun of him, but the grandiose spectacle of a man trying to stop the forces of nature with just a wet t-shirt got the better us. Even though he was nuts, he did not lack in courage or resolution, and I'd be proud to work with him again.

-Abner R.

Chapter 7

ISOLATED FINDS

When cultural materials are identified that don't meet the definition of an archaeological site, they are recorded as isolated finds. At *Shovel Bum*, we frequently get contributions that don't really fit the theme of a given issue. We include them anyway because their variety makes for a good read. This chapter collects together the wide range of isolated finds from the first eight issues of *Shovel Bum*.

April 5, 1953

Dear Doctor Krang,
    It is upon our recommendation
that your current NSF proposal concern-
ing "ro-botics" will not be funded. The
2 million grant will not be awarded to
a project involving ro-bots, or mechanical
men of any kind.
    Instead, the National Science
Foundation review board has awarded the
funding to an archaeological study that
will focus on the prehistory of uplands
Iowa. We sincerely hope that you find a
way to continue your research, as we at
NSF believe that ro-bots will one day be
important contributors to our modern
societies.
    Thank you for your interest in the

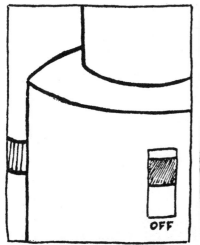

YES FELLOW SHOVELBUMS, SOONER OR LATER....

IT'S TIME FOR A PROFESSIONAL ARCHAEOLOGY CONFERENCE!

BY TROY '03

A HANDY GUIDE FOR ATTENDING CONFERENCES

AS WITH MOST THINGS IN THIS DISCIPLINE, YOU MUST ALSO CONSIDER THE BOTTOM LINE.

THE SELF FUNDED FIELD TECH OR STUDENT.

FINE LIVING ON THE UNIVERSITY'S DIME.

THIS IS ARCHAEOLOGY, SO DON'T OVERLOOK THE COST OF DRINKING!

FOUR BUCK BEERS IN THE HOTEL LOUNGE ARE A FACT OF LIFE.

BUT I ONCE SPIED A SHOVEL BUM PRACTICING THIS TRICK IN THE HOTEL LOBBY!

BOTTLE UP SLEEVE OF JACKET

GLASS FROM ROOM

ITS TAKEN FOR GRANTED THAT THE REAL WORKINGS OF ARCHAEOLOGY (FINDING EMPLOYMENT, AWARDING GRANTS, VERIFYING FINDS, DISMISSING GRADUATE STUDENTS, GOSSIPING ABOUT COLLEAGUES, ETC...) USUALLY OCCURS IN DARKLY LIT ROOMS.

BUT THIS SHOULDN'T STOP YOU FROM LEAVIN THE BAR AND ATT A FEW PAPERS.

PERUSE THE LIST OF PAPERS PROVIDED IN EXCHANGE FOR YOUR 125 BUCK REGISTRATION.

ALSO GOT SOUVENIR COFFEE MUG

CAREFULLY SELECT THE MOST PROMISING ABSTRACTS...

THEN WASTE 20 MINUTES WITH EACH, SINCE THE ABSTRACTS WERE WRITTEN 6 TO 8 MONTHS AGO — LONG BEFORE ANY RESEARCH WAS COMPLETED.

ACTUALLY, PREPARE TO WASTE 28 MINUTES SINCE THE WORST PRESENTERS INVARI- ABLY DRONE ON LONG PAST ANY TIME LIMITS.

CLICK!

IF YOU'RE ACTUALLY GIVING A PAPER, DON'T BOTHER CHECKING IF SLIDES ARE OUT OF ORDER, BACKWARD, OR UPSIDE- DOWN...

ANYBODY KNOW HOW THIS THING WORKS?

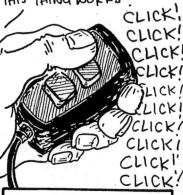

CLICK! CLICK! CLICK! CLICK! CLICK! CLICK! CLICK! CLICK! CLICK! CLICK!

YOU WOULDN'T WANT TO STAND OUT FROM ANY OTHER PRESENTERS.

BUT, WHATEVER TRANS- PIRES, DON'T WORRY. THIS IS AN ANNUAL CONFERENCE — THERE'S ALWAYS NEXT YEAR!

END!

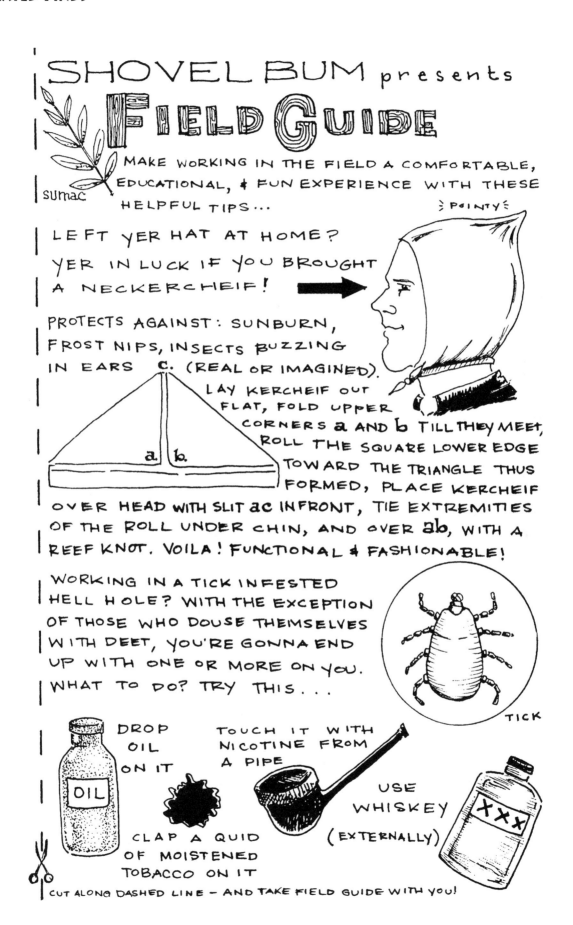

SHOVEL BUM presents

FIELD GUIDE

sumac

MAKE WORKING IN THE FIELD A COMFORTABLE, EDUCATIONAL, & FUN EXPERIENCE WITH THESE HELPFUL TIPS...

≥ POINTY ≥

LEFT YER HAT AT HOME?

YER IN LUCK IF YOU BROUGHT A NECKERCHEIF! ➡

PROTECTS AGAINST: SUNBURN, FROST NIPS, INSECTS BUZZING IN EARS C. (REAL OR IMAGINED).

LAY KERCHEIF OUT FLAT, FOLD UPPER CORNERS a AND b TILL THEY MEET, ROLL THE SQUARE LOWER EDGE TOWARD THE TRIANGLE THUS FORMED, PLACE KERCHEIF OVER HEAD WITH SLIT ac INFRONT, TIE EXTREMITIES OF THE ROLL UNDER CHIN, AND OVER ab, WITH A REEF KNOT. VOILA! FUNCTIONAL & FASHIONABLE!

a. b.

WORKING IN A TICK INFESTED HELL HOLE? WITH THE EXCEPTION OF THOSE WHO DOUSE THEMSELVES WITH DEET, YOU'RE GONNA END UP WITH ONE OR MORE ON YOU. WHAT TO DO? TRY THIS...

TICK

DROP OIL ON IT

OIL

CLAP A QUID OF MOISTENED TOBACCO ON IT

TOUCH IT WITH NICOTINE FROM A PIPE

USE WHISKEY (EXTERNALLY)

XXX

CUT ALONG DASHED LINE — AND TAKE FIELD GUIDE WITH YOU!

FIELD GUIDE CONT'D
tick removal cont'd

ONE CAN STAND NAKED IN THE DENSE SMOKE OF A GREEN WOOD FIRE (ALSO IS GOOD FOR THE PORES)

AS MOST KNOW, SEED TICKS ARE THE MOST DIFFICULT TO GET RID OF. IT ISN'T UNHEARD OF TO BE COVERED BY HUNDREDS OF THEM. IN SUCH A CASE, LET HIM STRIP AND RUB HIMSELF WITH KEROSENE.

THESE TIPS WERE GATHERED FROM THE ONE & ONLY ULTIMATE HANDBOOK, CAMPING AND WOODCRAFT BY HORACE KEPHART... GREAT VOCABULARY & ODD SYNTAX — COPYRIGHT 1917!

shovel bum's
SUPERFRIENDS

Ask any shovel bum what their trowel of choice is and undoubtedly they'll reply, "Marshalltown." Why Marshalltown? Try using an inferior company's trowel sometime and when the blade snaps off from the handle the first time you try to saw through a root, you'll know the answer. Marshalltowns are built tough and hold up against the extreme rigors of excavation. But how did Marshalltown rise to the top of the trowel industry? Let's examine their long and illustrious history.

The company started in (surprise!) Marshalltown, Iowa. Dave Lennox owned and operated his own machine shop in beautiful downtown Marshalltown and in 1893, he was approached by John Stine, a local stone mason who was looking for someone to build him *the* super trowel. Stine provided Lennox with several ideas and the first Marshalltown trowel was born. But Lennox quickly found the trowel-making business tiresome, so he turned the work over to two of his apprentices, E.L. and J.C. Williams (pictured below).

E.L Williams   J.C. Williams

Soon every stone mason in central Iowa was using the Williams brothers' trowels, and the demand was sufficient enough for the brothers to open their own machine shop. They continued to produce high quality trowels, selling them under the name, "Williams Brothers, Machinists." Business was good, but things really took off in 1905 when a smooth-talking, master salesman and promoter named Al Higgin took over the marketing side of the business. Higgin convinced the boys to change the name of the company to Marshalltown Trowel Company, and through his funding and several lucrative contacts, Higgin spread the Marshalltown name throughout the country.

Shovel Bum and the Accursed Egg

An ode to indie rockers of the High Plains
by Jason LaBelle

Soon enough, our crew will be in Yuma County, Colorado -- the veritable heartland of the Paleoindian world -- rocking out to the likes of AC/DC and Floyd. But perhaps the greatest thrill will be a pilgrimage to Jones-Miller and a little listen to the Hammer of the Gods. You know, you just can't find those Dandy Warhols on the AM dial out here.

Check out the Jan '79 issue of *National Geographic* at a garage sale or book store, as there is lots of cool stuff on Jones-Miller -- photos which inspired this campfire yarn (but don't miss the true gem of the issue, a little floppy black 33-1/3 recording of "Songs of the Humpback Whale." Talk about the good old days of free records in cereal and magazines...) So friends, here I give to you:

The Jones-Miller Shaman's Pole,
Sung to the Led Zep classic "Gallows Pole"

Women, children, hold that pen a while,
Think I see sister bison coming, run a many mile.

Friends, you get that whistle?
Did you get the li'l dog too?
What did you bring me, my dear friends, to the magic Shaman's Pole?
What did you bring me to keep me, atop that mighty smoking Pole?

I couldn't get no Edwards, I couldn't much 'Bates too,
You know we're so damn hungry, we need our cherished Pole

Women, children hold a little while.
I think I see our hunters coming, running a many mile.

Brother, did you get me some Smoky?
Did you get me some Flattop too?
What did you bring me, my brother, to call bison to the Shaman's Pole?

Brother, I brought you a whistle,
a butchered dog too, I brought a miniature Hell Gap point
To keep you working the cottonwood Pole.

Pronghorn, deer, turn your head awhile,
I think I see your sisters coming, slogging a many, mile, mile, mile.
Animals, I implore you, take them by the hand,
Take them to a deep snowdrift, save us from the wrath of this land.
Please take them, save us from the poverty of this land, land.

Women, children, upon your face a smile.
Pray tell me that we're free to feast,
Upon the hides of plenty proud beasts.

Oh, yes, they had a fine shaman, worked since long ago,
Since the days of when flint drew Super-Plano, hunters to that old arroyo,
Your family brought him music, your children's dog warmed his soul,
But now that the great feast is mighty over, they must move down the road.

Drift on, down the High Plains road.

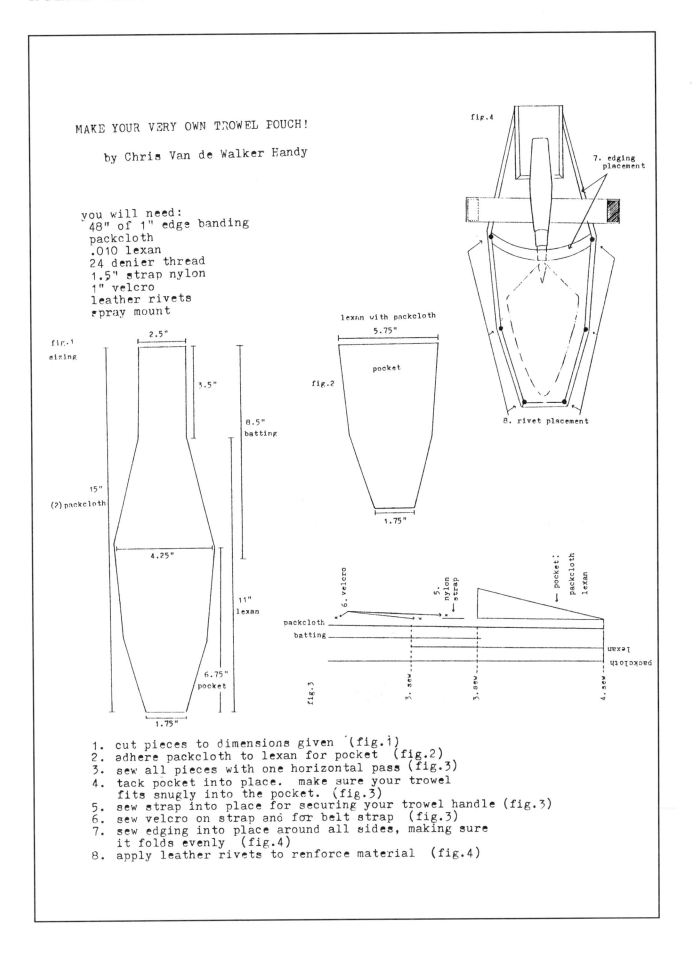

MAKE YOUR VERY OWN TROWEL POUCH!

by Chris Van de Walker Handy

you will need:
 48" of 1" edge banding
 packcloth
 .010 lexan
 24 denier thread
 1.5" strap nylon
 1" velcro
 leather rivets
 spray mount

fig.1
sizing

2.5"

3.5"

8.5"
batting

15"

(2) packcloth

4.25"

11"
lexan

6.75"
pocket

1.75"

lexan with packcloth
5.75"

pocket

fig.2

1.75"

fig.4

7. edging
placement

8. rivet placement

6. velcro

5. nylon strap

pocket:
packcloth
lexan

packcloth

batting

lexan

packcloth

3. sew

3. sew

4. sew

fig.3

1. cut pieces to dimensions given (fig.1)
2. adhere packcloth to lexan for pocket (fig.2)
3. sew all pieces with one horizontal pass (fig.3)
4. tack pocket into place. make sure your trowel
   fits snugly into the pocket. (fig.3)
5. sew strap into place for securing your trowel handle (fig.3)
6. sew velcro on strap and for belt strap (fig.3)
7. sew edging into place around all sides, making sure
   it folds evenly (fig.4)
8. apply leather rivets to renforce material (fig.4)

Chapter 8

GAMES

Crossword Puzzle, Duck
Unca T-Bone's Fieldwork Follies! Trent de Boer
Games, Betsy de Boer
Shovel Bum Superquiz, Trent de Boer
Crossword Puzzle, Duck
Not Getting Paid for Drive-time? Do Mad Lib! Cathy Bialas
How to Use the Tool! Troy Lovata
Games, Betsy de Boer
Cover art: Betsy de Boer

As one of our loyal *Shovel Bum* readers once pointed out, *Shovel Bum* is the perfect size to fit in a shovel bum's dig kit. This book is no exception. When we realized that our readers were taking their issues of *Shovel Bum* with them in the field, we decided to include archaeology-related games to challenge and entertain shovel bums during lunch breaks, drive time, and motel stays. Most veterans of the field shouldn't have difficulty with the following selections, but if you're stumped, e-mail us for the answers at dutchcircus@hotmail.com.

HORIZONTAL

1 CANADIAN SENTENCE ENDER

3 BRIEFS OFFER THIS, BOXERS DO NOT

7 "LET'S GET ___ WORK!"

8 MEXICO'S RULING PARTY (abbrv.)

9 CRM MAINSTAY (WITH HORIZONTAL #22)

11 ENJOY THIS COLD ONE AFTER WORK

12 WHAT A SCANNER DOES BEST

17 TWIST AN ANKLE? GOT SNAKE BIT? POKE YOURSELF WITH A TROWEL? BEFORE YOU SEE THE M.D. YOU'LL SEE THIS PERSON (abbrv.)

18 A GOOD SCRIBE'S QUILL HAS A SHARP ONE OF THESE

19 PROMINENT GEOLOGICAL FEATURE (abbrv.)

20 YOU CAN SPY ONE OF THESE ON CERTAIN MILITARY INSTALLATIONS

22 HAFT THIS ONTO YOUR SHAFT (W/HORIZONTAL #9)

25 NOT

26 "I'LL GO ___ OUT THE NEXT UNIT"

27 CATCH A MESS OF FISH WITH THESE CONTRAPTIONS

28 THESE DAYS THE GREAT BASIN IS JUST LOUSY WITH THESE FOLK (abbrv.)

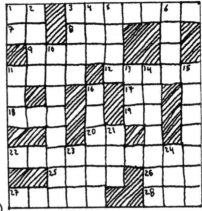

VERTICAL

1 SOME PEOPLE BELIEVE THE NAZCA LINES WERE BUILT BY ONE OR MORE OF THIS (abbrv.)

2 THESE FOLK HAVE RESERVATIONS ABOUT THE SOUTHWEST

3 A PINCH OF COPPENHAGEN MAKES SHOVEL BUM ___

4 Q: "WHAT'S A GREEK ___?"
A: "OH, ABOUT FIVE BUCKS AN HOUR."

5 SHOVEL BUM DIGS THESE

6 "*Rite in the* ___®"

10 SHOVEL BUM KNOWS THE HYPOTENUSE OF THIS IS 1.41 METERS. (3 wrds.)

11 SHOVEL BUM GROANS OVER THIS

13 IF YOU ARE A BUM WITH A SHOVEL WHAT CAREER SHOULD YOU SEEK? (abbrv.)

14 DURING PHASE I SHOVEL BUM CALL THIS NATURES BEAD STORE.

15 SHOVEL BUM USES CRITICAL EYES ON THESE

16 WHEN THINGS NEED PROBING TWIST THESE

21 SHOVEL BUM USES THIS ON HIS SORE MUSCLES "___ HOT"®

23 SHOVEL BUM KEEPS PICKLED EGGS IN THIS

24 A MAN IN A SKIRT CALLS A BOY BY THIS NAME

CROSSWORD
PUZZLE
BY
DUCK

*The answers can be found on page 42.

GAMES

Rebus Mania... DECIPHER THE PICTURES TO FIGURE OUT THE CLEVER PROPAGANDA. ANSWERS ON NEXT PAGE.

1.

2.

WHAT'S WRONG WITH THIS PICTURE?

Archaeologists rely on visual skills to identify artifacts. You can hone your skills by identifying the six differences betwixt the two illustrations at right.

SHOVEL BUM SUPERQUIZ

Okay, now here's a little quiz for all you self-styled shovel bum brainiacs. You know the deal -- answer the questions below to the best of your ability. The questions get progressively harder and only the most intelligent shovel bums will be able to answer all of the questions.

1/4"
1) What activities correspond to Phase I, II, and III archaeological projects?
2) How do you convert meters to feet?
3) Name three flake attributes.
4) What does P.I. stand for?
5) What is the English translation of per diem?

1/8"
6) What is the best way to deal with a poison ivy exposure?
7) What continent does kudzu originate from?
8) What country does cheatgrass originate from?
9) What is a pulaski?
10) What are preserved human feces called?

1/16"
11) What is the hypotenuse of a 50x50, a 1x1, and a 2x2?
12) In a 1x1, at what depth does OSHA require shoring?
13) When did the last ice age in North America end?
14) Where did beer, coffee, and cigarettes originate? (general region okay)
15) What color is 10YR7/3?

- If you answered 0-4 questions correctly, you are a greenhorn and probably need to spend more time in the field.
- If you answered 5-9 questions correctly, you've probably been in the lab or office too long. Get back in the field.
- If you answered 10-13 questions correctly, you're a shovel bum all right. Keep up the good work and you'll soon be able to answer all the questions.
- If you answered 14-15 questions correctly, you're a shovel bum brainiac! People look up to you for your leadership and knowledge. Hats off to you, champion.

ANSWERS:
1) Survey, Testing, Data Recovery 2) Multiply by 3.2808 3) Striking platform, bulb of percussion, dorsal surface, ventral surface, eraillure scar, hinge fracture, etc. 4) Principal Investigator 5) Each day 6) Soap and water 7) Asia 8) Portugal 9) A single-bit axe with an adze-shaped grub hoe extending from the back 10) Coprolites 11) 0.7071, 1.414, 2.828 12) About 4.5 meters 13) Around 12,000 years ago 14) Mesopotamia, Ethiopia, American Eastern Seaboard 15) Very pale brown.

TO HIDE FROM DANGER IS NOT TO ESCAPE IT.

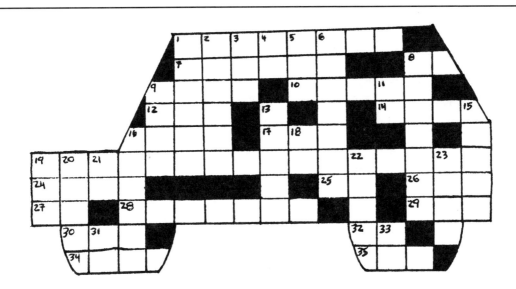

Cross Town Traffic

1. What the Swiss or the cowboys call singing.
7. Reparation for loss or injury.
8. This is the direction Shovel Bum walks 180° of NW.
9. To distort from a true value.
10. Shovel Bum will do this to an oyster.
12. "____-de-sac".
14. Shovel Bum's daily living allowance "per ___".
16. That which oozes.
17. An account set up independently by Shovel Bum for retirement purposes (abbrv.)
19. This particularly enjoyable geological phenomenon occurs when a largish land mass is relieved of its ice sheet (two words).
24. According to Blondie's song "Rapture," the man from Mars starts eating bars only after eating these.
25. City of Angels (abbrv.)
26. Slang for modern.
27. UFO pilot (abbrv.)
28. Hippy-type shovel bums burn this to get a fragrant smoke.
29. Protein rich bean (hint: not hempseed).
30. Mischievous fairy.
32. Her guidance counselor is a pimp.
34. Weeks are full of these.
35. Between projects, Shovel Bum can "____" out a living by hunting and gathering, temp work, unemployment insurance benefits, or rock hounding.

Down the Mountain

1. These mobsters use bullet trains.
2. To make this, Shovel Bum must get up early and crack a few eggs.
3. Morning condensation.
4. Spell the letter "N."
5. These folks may knock on your door and praise their tabernacle.
6. *Moby Dick's* narrator.
8. In winter, some shovel bums turn into these; turning in the trowel for a board or two.
9. This is exactly the type of guy who will wear a kilt.
11. Shovel Bum's lucky when the rental has an AM/FM radio with both cassette and "____".
13. Blood suckers!
15. Is it dirty water or watery dirt?
16. To turn to bone!
18. A road used by trains (abbrv.)
19. Solidified H_2O.
20. Satisfied.
21. The beaver state (abbrv.)
22. What Shovel Bum does in the bath tub.
23. This separates A.M. from P.M.
31. Charles Bukowski's city.
33. "____" Corral (abbrv.)

By Duck,
Shovel Bum
Puzzlemaster

Not getting paid for drive-time? Do Mad Lib!

It's _____ and ____ of us _____ into the
      time   #   Past tense verb

_____ to make the ____ hour drive to the project area.
 field vehicle   #

As we went along, _____ pointed out a strat of _____ ash
              crew member   name of volcano

in a road cut. _____ mumbled about _____ in
            crew member   Mexican dish

his/her sleep and drooled on _____'s _____.
                    crew member   body part

_____ was _____ driving ____ miles per hour up
 crew member   adverb   #

_____ pass, when the semi-truck ahead _____,
 mountain pass   past tense verb

spilling its cargo of _____ _____. We swerved and
          adjective   plural noun

nearly crashed into a _____ _____ with
          color   vehicle

_____ painted on its side. "Holy _____ Batman!",
 "South Park" character   last name of famous Archaeologist

cried _____.
    crew member

Crossing onto _____ land, _____ noticed the
       Federal Agency   crew member

rig was _____ _____. ____ tires were _____,
    "ing" verb adverb # between 1 and 4 adjective

and _____ rolled his/her _____ and pulled his/her
 field director   body part

_____. _____ dribbled onto the ground and into
 clothing article Vehicle fluid

the cache of _____ points that the rig was parked over. The sun
     projectile point type

_____ in a _____ sky over the cooling towers of
 past tense verb   color

_____, and we thought, "What a _____ job we have!"
 nuclear power plant   explicative

by C. Bialas, aka Nancy Drew, aka Qui

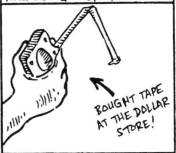

WORDSEARCH

```
I S O L A T E W I B X
D Y U C A R H A R T T
E G N U M V D L P B I
B D H K N T I C K E A
I R O P F T R O W E L
T L C A W S O Z K R H
A F J G X U L C A O I
G R S I A E P R D X Y
E P E R D I E M W L N
```

1. PER DIEM
2. CRM
3. TROWEL
4. DEBITAGE
5. BEER
6. CARHARTT
7. RIG
8. ISOLATE
9. SUUNTO
10. TICK

JUMBLE

```
G R I E A B N
○
```

TAKE THE LETTERS IN CIRCLES TO MAKE UP THE COMIC PUNCHLINE!

```
N E S C R E
  ○   ○
```

```
V O E L S H
          ○
```

```
E A T T N R S C
    ○
```

WHAT EVERY SHOVEL BUM HOPES FOR...

```
☐ ☐ ☐ ☐ ☐
```

PUTTING SHOVEL BUM IN CONTEXT: WHY A VIEW FROM THE SHOVEL HANDLE MATTERS

I must admit, being a frequent contributor to *Shovel Bum*, that I feel a bit reticent when I claim that it really means something. I feel the mighty push of ego when I come right out and state that a few dozen pages of images and text, cartoons even, actually matter. *Shovel Bum* is about archaeology and archaeology here in America has grown into an incredibly diverse discipline since Edgar Lee Hewett taught the first college level course specifically on the subject at New Mexico Highlands University in 1900. Archaeologists are an amiable lot—most of us wouldn't be involved in the field if we weren't—but, frankly, we rarely agree. The small forests of paper and hundreds of hours of documentary film expended on the subject each year are stark testament to our ability not only to find something new, but find fault with the old. One would be hard pressed to even identify a single textbook deemed satisfactory enough to start out the next generation. *Shovel Bum*, when weighed against this massive and chattering output, seems small indeed. Yet, when placed in context, one sees the power in its diminutive demeanor. When one begins to ask why such a publication exists, when one sees how it compares, when one understands that it tells much about the discipline—then it becomes very clear that *Shovel Bum* matters a lot.

Shovel Bum tells two stories. One is a tale of what it takes to move dirt, uncover artifacts, contemplate the past, and pay the rent. This is the story of the individuals who rarely get mentioned by name, but who, as Patty Jo Watson observed (1991:273), form, "an archaeological proletariat, who do most of the field and laboratory work carried out in this country." Theirs are indeed intriguing, important and, unfortunately, all too underreported stories. *Shovel Bum* captures their point of view, but it chronicles something else as well. It tells us about how archaeology actually works. It presents the process behind bold claims about the past and the artifacts we examine. Its very existence helps explain the state of the discipline. Understanding what *Shovel Bum* is about is to know how the field functions—who's who, how decisions are made, and who gets to decide.

Zines and Why There's One About Working at Archaeology

Shovel Bum is a zine. It's important to understand what this moniker means because it explains a lot about why there's a comic illustrated, sometimes humorous, sometimes snide publication concerned with the workings of archaeology. Zine is derived from fanzine, which is itself a contraction of fan magazine (Gunderloy and Janice 1992:2). Fanzines were amateur publications—as opposed to paying, professional magazines—originally produced by science fiction fans and date back to the golden age of 1930s and 1940s pulp sci-fi (Wright 2001:41). They were a medium in which fans could share their own stories, offer critical commentary, discuss the nuances and rules of sci-fi, and form a community of like minds. In the 1970s, following the blossoming of the underground press movement, fanzines grew to include music and movies—often in direct response to a perceived lack of adequate representation in the mainstream press for genres like slasher horror flicks and punk rock (Stoneman 2001:24). And then, sometime early in the Reagan years, a lot of people found a voice that had less to do with fan fawning and more connection to personal self-sufficiency and alternatives to the passive consumption of mass media (Duncombe 1997:40). When this was combined with the advent of cheap computers, accessible desktop publishing, and widely available photocopiers, zines grew into their own (Dodge 1995:27).

Zines are a place to record personal perspectives and personal lives outside the confines of market and profit motive (Dodge 1995:26). This separates zines from magazines because they aren't produced with the intention of filling a marketing niche or successfully selling advertising space to a particular demographic. Their perspective has run the gamut from politics to cultural scenes to diary-like chronicling of the mundane activities of day-to-day life (a slightly out of date, but nonetheless good introduction, to the sheer variety of topics zines address is found in Gunderloy and Janice's 1992 book *The World of Zines*—which was based on the now defunct *Factsheet Five*, a seminal and wildly successful zine dedicated simply to cataloging and chronicling other zines). Zines usually start with the work of an individual with individual interests, however wide or narrow they may be, and individual stories to tell (Duncombe 1997:9–10).

Yet, zines are significant because of their ability to form critical bridges between the individual and group. They are a medium in which the personal broadens into the community—a medium where people can share. When a zine lasts beyond a couple issues the individual often starts to give way to the multiple. People apart from the founder/publisher become contributors and not just ideas, but physical things are shared. Stephen Duncombe (1997:10) notes that, "the form of the zine lies somewhere between a personal letter and a magazine." Letter writing is an apt metaphor for the community zines can build because people interact and relationships are built through creative production. After reading a zine many people respond by crafting something of their own. They don't simply discuss what they've found in print. They often send in a submission or even publish their own zine in response (Stoneman 2001:34). The constructive reply includes the typical letter to the editor. But it can extend much further and build far stronger links between people when the response is creatively demanding enough to include hand-drawn pictures or offer a revealing personal narrative that includes one fessing up to both the good and bad within themselves (Wright 2001:48). Zines are ephemeral and rarely meet a strict publishing schedule. Nevertheless, the cycle of reading and response is powerful enough to truly form community bonds.

A perusal of the collected run of *Shovel Bum* gives a glimpse of this process at work. Archaeology field tech Trent "T-Bone" de Boer sat down during a cultural resource survey in the hinterlands of Arkansas and sketched out in his field notes what he was really doing apart from the grandiose exploration of the past. He considered how his chosen work affected his actions—who he talked to, how he dressed, what he ate, how he slept—and drew pictures. He contemplated the limitations of the disciplinary voice he was given—what he thought he could discuss in specific situations, what does and doesn't go into an archaeology report—and then drew some more. He photocopied the results and started handing them out to friends, archaeologists, and lay people alike, to help explain all that was this curious career path. Slowly, people took notice, traded copies with an even wider set of acquaintances, and mentioned his work in serious graduate school classes filled with future archaeologists as well as in the web-page ramblings of people who simply liked comics and interesting stories (Bushnell 2000a, 2000b). Other archaeologists noted that he was presenting a little recorded, but often mentioned, narrative that mirrored their own lives. They began comparing his takes to their experiences. Some felt an urge to respond in kind and pictures and words started arriving at T-Bone's doorstep. With each new issue produced something more was discussed, more people were involved, and more stories were told. Individual archaeologists were interacting with each other not because they worked in the same region, studied under the same mentors, examined similar artifacts, or asked the same questions about the past. They were forming relationships with each other because the very act of doing archaeology had shaped their lives. They came to know each other not through the typical disciplinary routes of networking. Instead, people who hadn't previously known each other formed bonds by stretching the definition of archaeology and archaeologist to include the fact that doing it as a job changes not only one's perspective on the past, but one's lifestyle.

It is at this point that the context for *Shovel Bum*, and the reason for its existence, becomes clearer. *Shovel Bum* is a zine about work. How one is able to talk about their work tells us a lot about how their chosen field operates. There's a tradition in the genre of zines to contemplate and write about work. Employment simply takes up too much of most people's lives to escape the introspective eye that zines offer (Duncombe 1997:73–74). Moreover, popular publications like *Temp Slave*, produced by the bourgeoning and often unwilling pool of temporary workers, or *Dishwasher*, which chronicled a single man's goal to wash dishes, don't merely consider employment as an aspect of one's life worth examination. They center themselves around the fact that people's jobs impact their entire lives. Likewise, the voice of a worker in archaeology, and how a zine about archaeology as a job is able to express it, can illuminate a lot about the way in which the discipline functions.

Stephen Duncombe (1997:74) notes that many zines approach work from the perspective that, "most people work for somebody else, producing or serving something over which they have little say, and doing it in a way that gives them little satisfaction." Archaeology as work is deep enough for this to occasionally both ring very true and fail to adequately describe the role of Patty

Jo Watson's (1991:273) "archaeological proletariat." There is a choice to pursue archaeology as a career, yet there is also a reality that the majority of what archaeologists actually do is very different from what they're prepared to do in school or what they can emulate from the discipline's past and present giants. This is not to say that one career path is worth privileging over another, just that there are noticeable differences between the academic as scholar, the academic as student, the field worker as manager, and the field worker as technician (Russell 1996:130–131, Watson 1991:272–273). *Shovel Bum* is about negotiating these differences. Archaeology is, of course, different from other jobs and archaeologists do have some choice and say. The ability to work not just to pay the bills, but to interact with something as enticing as the past attracts many to this discipline. Archaeology can be an extremely satisfying profession. However, shovel bums are, as a lot, the students and technicians who generate primary data and write field reports, but don't always get to decide what data is worth looking for and don't always get first, or even third, author credit. Moreover, archaeologists at all levels are often the last to decide where they physically work and they do actually work for someone else; whether it be an educational institution with its administrators and regents, a contract firm with its accountants and profit motive, or any other of the myriad of positions, with their particular limitations, in which archaeologists are found. What *Shovel Bum* does is talk about, and illustrate, what doesn't get put into much of the rest of written archaeological discourse. It considers more than what was uncovered and what that might tell us about the past. It considers the above-mentioned facts that someone else may be controlling the money, that archaeologists are employees, and that our lives are affected not just by the choice to do archaeology, but other's choices about the field.

Ian Hodder (1995:264–265) noted nearly a decade ago that modern archaeological writing leaves out significant description of what happened in the process of uncovering things about the past. His examination of how the discipline's writing has changed over the past few hundred years shows a trend away from, "emphases on the 'I', the actor, dialogue, narrative sequence and interpretation tied to the contingent context of discovery . . ." (Hodder 1995:268). Modern archaeologists communicate with each other and understand the past primarily through the interpretation of the written word (Boivin 1997:105). Yet, modern professional discourse is now a very formalized means of communication, in which:

> The writing has become increasingly distant, objective, impersonal and universal. We have become blind to the fact that we are writing. It appears as if self-evident data are described in neutral terms. The description is undated, timeless and beyond history (Hodder 1995:269).

There is, of course, reason that this format developed and there are many claims to be made about standardizing or coding data for use by others (Hodder 1995:271; Stevens 1997:130–132). Nevertheless, whether you agree or not with Ian Hodder (1995:264–265) and Jeremy Sabloff (1999:871) that it isn't just the rigorous application of scientific discipline that has formalized writing, it is clear that professional communication within archaeology is more detached than it used to be.

Archaeology's formalized structure of communication also tends to neglect the collective nature of archaeological research and the fact that numerous individuals contributed to the collection, interpretation and publication of any story about the past (Hodder 1995:269). However, this is where modern professional writing doesn't differ with the past to any great extent. Authorship is still cited and credit is still given primarily to the individuals in charge. Narrative accounts from previous generations were first person descriptions, but that first person was all too often the director and not the individuals who actually moved the dirt. The examples of professional writing that Ian Hodder (1995:263, 267) examined from archaeology's distant past do make subjective note of time, date, and circumstance. However, the laborers who took shovels in hand are unnamed figures, sometimes not even referred to as individuals. They lack the opportunity to describe what it was like to uncover evidence and what choices they made in their labors, much less discuss what it meant to be ordered to dig.

Shovel Bum's perspective on archaeology as work is different both from much of what has come before and much of what is currently considered the discipline's standard. Ian Hodder (1997:265) notes that much of archaeology's early writing took the form of correspondence and letters filled with the subjectivity of first person accounts. This is an interesting comparison to Stephen Duncombe's observation (1997:10) that zines like *Shovel Bum* are something akin to a personal letter. Jeremy Bushnell (2000b) observes that, "providing 'human context' is one of the things that zines do best, and *Shovel Bum* is no exception." However, *Shovel Bum* is also distinct because is doesn't just provide the context through which one can better understand artifacts or the story of the past. It presents narratives from a different class of archaeologists. It is a consideration of the context of discovery in its own right. In fact, its view that archaeology is actually work, and that doing such work will shape one's entire lifestyle, separates *Shovel Bum* from other forms of disciplinary expression. Having said this, I must admit that it isn't the only attempt to express how archaeology functions or how it affects those who work at it—others have tried in their own way to capture some picture of what's going on (usually in 'state of the field' type articles like Stephen Black's 1995 review of Texas archaeology) and still more will attempt to explain as much in the future. As a contributor to a zine that builds networks based on these topics, I say the more the merrier. But *Shovel Bum* is different from most attempts at professional communication—even though Black's 1995 review mentions the need to better train students to successfully find employment as archaeologists, it never gets to the point of discussing how to handle per diem or what one eats in the field—and this helps explain what it is and why it exists. *Shovel Bum* exists, in part, because a few archaeologists have found a way to interact with each other based on what it means to work in their profession.

A Narrative that Matters

Shovel Bum's unique perspective on what gets archaeology done and how it changes a worker's life sets its place within the field. One can see why it exists. But it also actually matters. Works like *Shovel Bum*, which present a narrative of discovery and employment, are a necessary part of satisfying the discipline's responsibilities to itself and the public it serves. The topics it explores are often accounts of the day-to-day and the seemingly mundane in contrast to allure of shiny artifacts, exotic peoples who acted differently than we do, or mysteries of entire cultures undergoing change. But the chronicling of quotidian events is crucial for the discipline to explain itself to a wider audience and legitimate the accuracy and authority of the stories it tells about the past. *Shovel Bum* is small in size and the number of individual stories presented within it, from taking emergency shelter during survey, to deciding where to eat, to wrecking a company vehicle, is limited. Again, as a contributor to *Shovel Bum*, I don't mean to claim too much—it will never capture the full range of every archaeological outing. But it does form a necessary part of what needs to be published.

There are few professionals who would doubt archaeology's self-interest in successfully communicating with the public. Simon James (1992:306) and Jeremy Sabloff (1999:873) are but two who note that the preservation of sites and artifacts, the opportunity to present our findings, and the economic basis of our very employment are all balanced on our ability to positively influence a wide audience. It's all too clear that without successful public outreach the funding dries up and we can no longer work at our profession (Young 2002:240). But we have more than a self-interest in public communication; we have a responsibility to participate in a public archaeology because, at the end of the day, shovel bum and project director alike serve those outside our field. Poirier and Feder (1995:4) are right to claim it requisite that professionals cultivate, "an archeology open and accessible to the public, not just paid for by them." The past is a resource held by professionals in the public trust and we enshrine our responsibilities in our professional society's codes of conduct (Dunnell 1984:66, Kintigh 1996:5, 17).

Archaeologists study the lives of real people. Therefore, they rarely face a disinterested public because everyone has direct connection, both legally (Carnett 1991:11) and emotionally (Bender 1998:64), to some part of the past. Public opinion surveys have repeatedly confirmed the high level of interest in not just the past, but archaeology as a discipline (including, among others, Feder 1987, 1995; Harrold and Eve 1987; Lovata and Benitez 1999, Pokotylo and Guppy 1999; and Taylor 1995). Stephen Williams (1987:131) does not overstate himself when declaring that, "all in all, we have a good product to sell—archaeology is a fascinating subject and viewed as such by millions of people."

But neither the high-minded sentiment of a resource held in the public trust nor the self-interest in being able to keep doing what we do means that we're particularly successful in our attempts at a public archaeology. William Lipe (2002:20) has observed that, "the benefits of archaeological research are often not directly accessible to the public because the work is highly technical, and research results are generally published in books and articles written primarily for other archaeologists." And Francis McManamon (1997:2) reminds us that, "the shorthand of archaeological jargon and densely written professional material makes poor fare for reaching out to anyone." Moreover, professional codes of conduct only deem it necessary that we professionally and publicly present our findings and what we know about the past (Kintigh 1996:17). Neither these codes nor many archaeologists themselves have always recognized the necessity to widely report not just what they uncover, but the processes by which they operate.

Providing not just a catalog of finds, but a narrative describing how we go about our work is an essential part of communicating with the public (Lovata 2000:96). On one hand, people like William Lipe (2002:24) note that, "the dynamic character of archaeological research has the potential to help make archaeology more interesting to the public." Simply explaining how archaeology operates drives much of the relationship between professional and public. The previously mentioned opinion polls are telling. Archaeologists are continually approached by strangers at cocktail parties and in public places because people want to know something not only about the past, but how we came to understand it (Stiebing 1987:9; Young 2002:240). When we fail to include a narrative of what we do, we fail to connect. Archaeologist Nicole Boivin (1997:110) declares that:

> Archaeology *is* an interesting subject . . . How can such dried up and shriveled accounts have been born of a tree that is so majestic and exotic? How is it that individuals who regularly visit exotic locales, who pay live witness to the extravagances of beauty and horror that typify the human species, who pursue the mysteries and unearth that which has been lost forever, who operate at the crux of the coming together of a babbling multitude of diverse disciplines . . . how is it that they of all people can produce as their end results and final conclusions such desiccated and anemic summaries? Surely the sin of dullness is a hundred-fold multiplied when it is perpetrated by the archaeologist.

Peter Young, publisher of the popular magazine *Archaeology*, offers a similar sentiment when he suggests that archaeologists need to be better storytellers. He (Young 2002:240) laments the fact that too many manuscripts arrive at his office, "bone dry and bloodless." Peter Young's (2002:242) advice to writers is to, "keep it personal without being egocentric," because, "readers are interested in you and the story that is unfolding; they should be led through your material . . ." They should be given a narrative.

Quality storytelling and interesting descriptions of work in progress are powerful steps in public communication. *Shovel Bum* is significant because it has generated positive reviews for the way it tells stories (Bushnell 2000a, 2000b). It does generate public interest (it is being collected in this anthology, after all) and this won't be the end for its creators—if nothing else it could be viewed as practice on the road to better storytelling. But Chris Stevens (1997:130, 137), in reply to Nicole Boivin's lament on the sins of boring writing, makes a valid point when he notes that exciting stories go only so far. If successfully generating public interest was a goal unto itself, I would not be so adamant in the belief that *Shovel Bum* matters. In fact, I believe that something much larger is at stake. Without a discussion of how archaeology gets done—including the mundane tribulations we face, the complaints we have about the system, the alternating cycles of boredom and awe we go through, and the gripes we have about each other—the discipline risks its ability to speak with authority about the past. Without a successful presentation of our means and methods we risk losing out to, among others, the Creationists, pseudoscientists and New Age theorists. These are real threats to our ability not only to thrive, but meet our responsibilities to the past (Sabloff 1999:869, 873). William Lipe (2002:24, 26) notes that most of our discipline's failings to counter fantastic and false claims are directly related to our inability to show the public how the past is constructed. This includes our disagreements and the changes both the discipline and we as individuals go through. William Stiebing Jr. (1987:8–9) observes that:

Anthropologists, archaeologists, and historians should learn from [the] controversy over evolution and creationism, for the average lay person doesn't really understand the methodology of the social sciences either. Laymen think of the past in terms of "facts." By digging in the ground or rummaging through old documents, scholars discover these "facts." But few people understand the details of how this process works . . . If we spent a little more time making our methodology understandable, maybe the public would be able to recognize the problems that characterize cult archaeology without professional help.

When we fail to creatively discuss our work as work, we fail at much more than being interesting.

Words Can Be Funny, Pictures Can Be Important

Shovel Bum's pages are filled with a distinct discussion of what it means to do archaeology. This makes it important. But it's not just what's discussed that makes it matter—it's how it's being done. *Shovel Bum* uses a lot of pictures along with its words—funny pictures. It's comic illustrated and it's often quite irreverent, if not downright humorous. Haiku odes to the broken down motels that archaeologists stay in. Contemplating the coolness of driving up to camp in a dump truck. Considering what robot diggers would look like. Filling out Mad-Libs about faulty field vehicles. These things are funny. Drawings of stick figure quality with just enough hair-related attributes to identify the real people behind them. One-inch square thumbnails of motel room accidents. Pictures of measuring tapes injecting performance-enhancing steroids. A photograph of *Shovel Bum* covers plastered over the service entrance of the American Museum of Natural History. These things are intriguing to look at. They are of a quality that drives the readers of *Shovel Bum* to participate in the creative cycle of response and reply that underlies a zine built community. However, these are also very significant things as archaeology presents itself to the public and attempts to thrive. Publications like *Shovel Bum* work toward filling a very real need for humorous ideas and funny pictures.

Archaeologists are a visual lot. We make sketches in our field notes that are both necessary (think soil profiles) and otherwise (consider the caricatures of the boss's hippy haircut and shaggy mustache). We're entranced by the physical shape of artifacts and their appearance as potent symbols of the past (Warburton and Duke 1995:211–213). People use images as a stockpile of memes with which we can approach new situations and compare to what we already know (Greenblatt 1991:6–7). Archaeologists are no different. We've judged the validity of claims about the past based on the drawings we produce (Van Reybrouck 1998). Stephanie Moser (1998:18) and Simon James (1997:34) are but two who have documented our tendency to discuss the past with the subtle subtext of images that shape our opinions about what is right and what is wrong. Publisher Mitch Allen (2003:6) observes that, even when archaeologists don't have useful drawings or explanatory pictures, they still submit piles of photographs along with every manuscript.

Yet, for all our attraction to images, the academic environment of archaeology actually neglects, if not acts prejudiced against, visual communication. The same people who document the power of pictures repeatedly note that such power is discounted and ignored (Bradley 1997:62; James 1997:24). Simon James (1997:24) and Brian Molyneaux (1997:1) observe that in our rush to describe the past in the elite jargon of detached, objective wording, professionals have the propensity to consider images the domain of children and the uneducated. There have been times when I've shown my own comics to particular colleagues that I've felt the disregard that Jeremy Sabloff (1999:873–874) finds endemic to academia. Some like what they see. Some note that such pictures have captured something all too human and fragile about the discipline. But, even though the ability to create such images requires careful preparation and understanding of the issues, some fail to appreciate how necessary images are.

Comics are powerful. Their ability to amplify by simplifying, to distill an essence of an issue, and to juxtapose important concepts is perhaps unrivaled (Lovata 2000:7–8). Bill Sillar (1992:209–210) has shown how devastatingly effective the juxtaposition of a simple cartoon about prehistory against many, many pages of critical text can be at exposing fallacious thinking. So many of Gary Larson's "Far Side" cartoons were taped upon so many archaeologist's office doors because they were so efficient at capturing our basest instincts. Jeremy Sabloff (1999:869) was certainly not the first professional or scientist to use a "Far Side" cartoon to explain what's wrong with their discipline. Even if all one can do is draw figures a level little above stickmen, these are cartoons worth emulating.

Of course, it's not just any kind of image that exhibits such power. It's the funny or satirical images that shake us. Philip Rahtz and Ian Burrows (1992:373) have declared that, "archaeology is too important a subject not to be joked about." They understand that there's nothing like an amusing and satirical cartoon to reach a tentative audience, make a serious point palatable, critique earlier people and institutions (including the ones we study), or expose intolerant theory for what it is (Rahtz and Burrows 1992:373). Bill Sillar (1992:205–206) explains that, "humour is a rhetorical weapon from which there is no easy defense," because it opens your eyes to new viewpoints by, "asking you to look at the familiar from a different angle, frequently inviting you to laugh at what you might otherwise take for granted, or pass by unnoticed." Self-parody and satire are as important as clear narratives in countering the processes of ambivalent elitism and the vilification of the establishment as dogmatic that allows cult archaeology, New Age theories, and pseudoscientific explanations about the past to thrive (Stiebing 1987:4–6). By laughing at ourselves we are human and reachable. By laughing at ourselves we show how laughable the idea is that we're closed minded academics, colonial plunderers, treasure-happy gold diggers, or cultural scrooges who covet and hide the truth for no one but ourselves. Dictators of all stripes are unable to laugh at themselves. Bill Sillar (1992:207) makes a plea for more comics because they expose the incongruity of belief in both the past and present. *Shovel Bum* is important because it tries to answer this call.

Youth

In the end, a lot of what *Shovel Bum* is able to do is connected to youth. Its writers can discuss the way archaeology functions and look at what they're doing as work because they were new enough to the field to still compare it to what they've done before. They're close enough to being, if not still are, students and, therefore, they're practiced at asking "why?" They're open to building a network with each other because they know what it's like to be excluded from decision making and the means of production. They know what mainstream domination means and respect the ability to tell an individual story in an intimate format. They are knowledgeable of what a zine can offer. This is why Nicole Boivin (1997:115) feels that those on the low end of the academic totem pole (the graduate students, young researchers, and the like), "who have the least vested interest in maintaining the status quo," are the most likely to make archaeology and archaeological writing interesting. She (Boivin 1997:115) notes that though one would expect that long-standing and tenured academics can get away with advocating change— they could offer interesting formulations and radical critique because they've less on the line than people under review and moving from job to job—that the system is just too entrenched for them to act. In many ways it seems up to youth. Anthropologist Julie Chu (1997) has produced a particularly vivid portrait of how youths use zines to claim a place within the media environment. She (Chu 1997:83) explains how, "the media as an environment for youths looks tremendously different and *richer* when zine publisher's own perceptions are center stage." Her work shows that zines can make things relevant and make things happen for a young generation (Chu 1997:77–78). Chu (1997:82–83) perceptively asks not how people can dictate to the next generation, but, "how *we can involve ourselves* in the projects young people are initiating on their own."

But labeling *Shovel Bum*, or any other zine, as simply a product of youth is too dismissive. I've heard people write off *Shovel Bum* as a graduate school lark. I've heard them imply that comics and humor are not what professionals do. This type of criticism raises my hackles. It's the kind of trivialization of any writing not expressively dry and detached that Jeremy Sabloff (1999:874) sees as squashing archaeology's ability to thrive. Sabloff has been the editor of a peer-reviewed, traditional journal and has served on many tenure committees, and he notes that too many of these established academic mechanisms are far too dismissive of alternative paths of communication that occasionally reach broad audiences (1999:873–874). It's true that both Trent "T-Bone" de Boer and myself, along with many other contributors, were in graduate school when *Shovel Bum* got underway. But that was nearly six years ago. Today, Trent is a project archaeologist for a respected firm with a Master's degree and years of experience in a field in which few last beyond their second season. I finished my doctorate nearly three years ago and am an Assistant Professor well on my way toward tenure at a flagship state university. I bring these facts up not to brag about our accomplishments, but to point out that we, and others, are still contributing to *Shovel Bum* when we could have easily moved on to more familiar academic writing. Yet, we're still drawing comics about being in the field because we still feel it worthwhile. We continue to believe it necessary to discuss our work in the way we do. Stephen Duncombe (1997:94) may explain some of this sentiment when he notes that:

The reality of work in a capitalist society may be dispiriting, but people are not so easily dispirited. Between the cracks of the system new—and very old—ideas and ideals of what work should be emerge. Zines are a medium through which to express these new ideals but, more important, they are actual embodiments of a type of work and creation that runs counter to the norm within our capitalist society.

These are pretty high ideals to live up to. Frankly, they're on the level of poignant cartoons that Gary Larson was able to produce in the "Far Side," and I'm not sure I'll ever reach those towering heights. And that is not only why Shovel Bum actually matters, but why I hope you'll enjoy it, think about what it means, and, maybe, draw a few cartoons of your own.

References

Allen, M.
    2003   *Field Guide to Archaeological Publishing. The SAA Archaeological Record.* 3(1):5–6.

Bender, B.
    1998   *Stonehenge: Making Space.* Berg, Oxford, England.

Black, S. L.
    1995   (Texas) Archeology 1995. *Bulletin of the Texas Archeological Society.* 66:17–45.

Boivin, N.
    1997   Insidious or Just Boring? An Examination of Academic Writing in Archaeology. *Archaeological Review from Cambridge.* 14(2):105–125.

Bradley, R.
    1997   'To see is to have seen'. In *The Cultural Life of Images.* B.L. Molyneaux, editor, Routledge, London, England.

Bushnell, J.P.
    2000a   *Shovel Bum #1. Invisible City Productions, Zine Reviews: February 2000.* http://www.invisible-city.com/zines/reviews200.htm#shove.
    2000b   *Shovel Bum #3. Invisible City Productions, Zine Reviews: February 2000.* http://www.invisible-city.com/zines/reviews200.htm#shove3.

Carnett, C.
    1991   *Legal Background of Archaeological Resources Protection.* Technical Brief No. 11, U.S. Department of the Interior, National Park Service, Washington, D.C.

Chu, J.
    1997   Navigating the Media Environment: How Youth Claim a Place Through Zines. *Social Justice.* 24(3):71–85.

Dodge, C.
    1995   Zines and Libraries: Pushing the Boundaries. *Wilson Library Bulletin.* 69(9):26–30.

Duncombe, S.
    1997   *Notes From Underground: Zines and the Politics of Alternative Culture.* Verso, London, England.

Dunnell, R.C.
    1984   The Ethics of Archaeological Significant Decisions. In *Ethics and Values in Archaeology.* E.L. Green, editor, Plenum Press, New York.

Feder, K.L.
    1987   Cult Archaeology and Creationism: A Coordinated Research Project. In *Cult Archaeology and Creationism.* F.B. Harrold and R.A. Eve, editors, University of Iowa Press, Iowa City.
    1995   Ten Years After: Surveying Misconceptions about the Human Past. *CRM.* 18(3):10–14.

Gunderloy, M. and C. Goldberg Janice
    1992   *The World of Zines: A Guide to the Independent Magazine Revolution*. Penguin Books, New York.

Harrold, F.B. and R.A. Eve
    1997   Patterns of Creationist Beliefs among College Students. In *Cult Archaeology and Creationism*. F.B. Harrold and R.A. Eve, editors, University of Iowa Press, Iowa City.

Hodder, I.
    1995   *Theory and Practice in Archaeology*. Routledge, London, England.

James, S.
    1992   'But Seriously Though, Folks' Humour, Archeology and Communication: The View from the Trenches. *Archaeological Review from Cambridge*. 11(2):299–309.
    1997   Drawing Inferences: Visual Reconstructions in Theory and Practice. In *The Cultural Life of Images*. B.L. Molyneaux, editor, Routledge, London, England.

Kintigh, K.W.
    1996   SAA Principles of Archaeological Ethics. *SAA Bulletin*. 14(3):5, 17.

Lipe, W.D.
    2002   Public Benefits of Archaeological Research. In *Public Benefits of Archeology*. B. Little, editor, University Press of Florida, Gainesville.

Lovata, T.R.
    2000   An Exploration of Archaeological Representation: People and the Domestic Dog on the Great Plains of North America. Doctoral Dissertation in the Department of Anthropology, The University of Texas, Austin.

Lovata, T.R. and A.V. Benitez
    1999   Does Anyone Really Know What You're Up To?: An Archaeological Survey. Paper presented at the 64th Annual Meeting of the Society for American Archaeology, Chicago, Illinois, March 29th, 1999.

McManamon, F.P.
    1997   Why Consult? *Common Ground*. Summer/Fall:2.

Molyneaux, B.L.
    1997   *The Cultural Life of Images*. Routledge, London, England.

Moser, S.
    1998   *Ancestral Images*. Cornell University Press, Ithaca, New York.

Poireir, D.A. and K.L. Feder
    1995   Sharing the Past with the Present. *CRM*. 18(3):3–4.

Pokotylo, D. and N. Guppy
    1999   Public Opinion and Archaeological Heritage: Views from Outside the Profession. *American Antiquity*. 64(3):400–416.

Russell, S. A.
    1996   *When the Land Was Young: Reflections on American Archaeology*. University of Nebraska Press, Lincoln.

Sabloff, J.
    1999   Distinguished Lecture in Archaeology: Communication and the Future of American Archaeology. *American Anthropologist*. 100(4):869–875.

Sillar, B.
    1992   Digging for a Laugh: Archaeology and humor. *Archaeological Review from Cambridge*. 11(2):203–211.

Stiebing Jr., W.H.
1987   The Nature and Dangers of Cult Archaeology. In *Cult Archaeology and Creationism*. F.B. Harrold and R.A. Eve, editors. University of Iowa Press, Iowa City.

Stevens, C.
1997   Is Academic Archaeological Writing Boring? Maybe. Uninteresting? Never. *Archaeological Review from Cambridge*. 14(2):127–140.

Stoneman, P.
2001   *Fanzines: Their Production, Culture and Future*. Master's Thesis in Publishing Studies, University of Stirling, Scotland.

Taylor, J.H.
1995   Why Creationists Don't Go to Psychic Fairs: Differential Sources of Pseudoscientific Belief. *Skeptical Inquirer*. 19(6):233–26.

Van Reybrouck, D.
1998   Imaging and Imagining the Neanderthal: The Role of Technical Drawings in Archaeology. *Antiquity*. 72:56–64.

Warburton, M. and P.J. Duke
1995   Projectile Points as Cultural Symbols. In *Beyond Subsistence: Plains Archaeology and the Post-Processual Critique*. P.G. Duke, editor, University of Alabama Press, Tuscaloosa.

Watson, P. J.
1991   A Parochial Primer: The New Dissonance as Seen from the Midcontinental United States. In *Processual and Postprocessual Archaeologies: Multiple Ways of Knowing the Past*. Robert W. Preucel, editor. Center for Archaeological Investigations, Southern Illinois University at Carbondale.

Williams, S.
1987   Fantastic Archaeology: What Should We Do About It? In *Cult Archaeology and Creationism*. F.B. Harrold and R.A. Eve, editors. University of Iowa Press, Iowa City.

Wright, F.A.
2001   *From Zines to Ezines: Electronic Publishing and the Literary Underground*. Doctoral Dissertation in the Department of English, Kent State University, Ohio.

Young, P.
2002   The Archaeologist as Storyteller. In *Public Benefits of Archeology*. B. Little, editor, University Press of Florida, Gainesville.

ABOUT THE AUTHOR

Trent de Boer is currently employed as an archaeologist for the Washington State Department of
Transportation. When Mr. de Boer is not off working
in some far-flung location, he enjoys spending time with
his wife, Betsy, and engaging in non-archaeology related
activities.